Yellow

by Del Shores

A Samuel French Acting Edition

SAMUELFRENCH.COM

Copyright © 2013 by Del Shores

ALL RIGHTS RESERVED

Author photo (back cover)© Alan Mercer
"Yellow" graphic (front cover) by Del Shores

CAUTION: Professionals and amateurs are hereby warned that *YELLOW* is subject to a licensing fee. It is fully protected under the copyright laws of the United States of America, the British Commonwealth, including Canada, and all other countries of the Copyright Union. All rights, including professional, amateur, motion picture, recitation, lecturing, public reading, radio broadcasting, television and the rights of translation into foreign languages are strictly reserved. In its present form the play is dedicated to the reading public only.

The amateur and professional live stage performance rights to *YELLOW* are controlled exclusively by Samuel French, Inc., and licensing arrangements and performance licenses must be secured well in advance of presentation. PLEASE NOTE that amateur licensing fees are set upon application in accordance with your producing circumstances. When applying for a licensing quotation and a performance license please give us the number of performances intended, dates of production, your seating capacity and admission fee. Licensing fees are payable one week before the opening performance of the play to Samuel French, Inc., at 45 W. 25th Street, New York, NY 10010.

Licensing fee of the required amount must be paid whether the play is presented for charity or gain and whether or not admission is charged.

Professional/Stock licensing fees quoted upon application to Samuel French, Inc.

For all other rights than those stipulated above, apply to: The William Morris Agency, LLC, 1325 Avenue of the Americas, New York, NY 10019; Attn.: Derek Zasky.

Particular emphasis is laid on the question of amateur or professional readings, permission and terms for which must be secured in writing from Samuel French, Inc.

Copying from this book in whole or in part is strictly forbidden by law, and the right of performance is not transferable.

Whenever the play is produced the following notice must appear on all programs, printing and advertising for the play: "Produced by special arrangement with Samuel French, Inc."

Due authorship credit must be given on all programs, printing and advertising for the play.

ISBN 978-0-573-70097-2   Printed in U.S.A.   #20496

No one shall commit or authorize any act or omission by which the copyright of, or the right to copyright, this play may be impaired.

No one shall make any changes in this play for the purpose of production.

Publication of this play does not imply availability for performance. Both amateurs and professionals considering a production are strongly advised in their own interests to apply to Samuel French, Inc., for written permission before starting rehearsals, advertising, or booking a theatre.

No part of this book may be reproduced, stored in a retrieval system, or transmitted in any form, by any means, now known or yet to be invented, including mechanical, electronic, photocopying, recording, videotaping, or otherwise, without the prior written permission of the publisher.

MUSIC USE NOTE

Licensees are solely responsible for obtaining formal written permission from copyright owners to use copyrighted music in the performance of this play and are strongly cautioned to do so. If no such permission is obtained by the licensee, then the licensee must use only original music that the licensee owns and controls. Licensees are solely responsible and liable for all music clearances and shall indemnify the copyright owners of the play and their licensing agent, Samuel French, Inc., against any costs, expenses, losses and liabilities arising from the use of music by licensees.

IMPORTANT BILLING AND CREDIT REQUIREMENTS

All producers of *YELLOW must* give credit to the Author of the Play in all programs distributed in connection with performances of the Play, and in all instances in which the title of the Play appears for the purposes of advertising, publicizing or otherwise exploiting the Play and/or a production. The name of the Author *must* appear on a separate line on which no other name appears, immediately following the title and *must* appear in size of type not less than fifty percent of the size of the title type.

In addition the following credit must be given in all programs and publicity information distributed in association with this piece:

Originally produced at The Coast Playhouse, West Hollywood, CA by Louise H. Beard, Emerson Collins, Jason Dottley and Del Shores

YELLOW was originally produced by Louise H. Beard, Emerson Collins, Jason Dottley, and Del Shores for JD3atrical at The Coast Playhouse in West Hollywood, California on June 11, 2010. It was directed by Del Shores; the set was by Robert Steinberg; set construction by Jeff Robinson; the lights were by Kathi O'Donohue; the sound was by Drew Dalzell and Mark Johnson. Musical arrangements were by Joe Patrick Ward; choreography was by Louise H. Beard; the costume design was by Craig Taggart. Casting was by Rich Delia; photography was by Brian Putnam and Rosemary Alexander; graphic design was by Jason Dottley; publicity was by David Elzer/DEMAND PR. The stage manager was Craig Taggart; the assistant stage managers were T. Ashanti Mozelle and Chris Pudlo. The original cast, in order of appearance, was as follows:

BOBBY WESTMORELAND . . . . David Cowgill
KATE WESTMORELAND . . . . Kristen McCullough
DAYNE WESTMORELAND . . . . Luke McClure
GRACIE WESTMORELAND . . . . Evie Louise Thompson
KENDALL PARKER . . . . Matthew Scott Montgomery
SISTER TIMOTHEA PARKER . . . . Susan Leslie

Important and appreciated appearances during the run were:

Rachel Sorsa (shared the role of **KATE**), Robert Lewis Stephenson and David Steen (**BOBBY**), Brett Fleisher (**DAYNE**), Caroline Shores (**GRACIE**), Kinna McInroe, and Madonna Cacciatore (**TIMOTHEA**).

Additional voices were: Rosemary Alexander, David Steen, David Cowgill, Ted Detwiler, Wyatt Earp, Tate Taylor, and Newell Alexander.

Pre-show dialogue and music was by Levi Kreis.

The singing waiters and cast of *Oklahoma* were: Rosemary Alexander, Emerson Collins, Rachel Sorsa, Kinna McInroe, Luke Stratte-McClure, Matthew Scott Montgomery, Del Shores, and Craig Taggart.

CHARACTERS

BOBBY WESTMORELAND – 40's. A football coach and family man. Easy-going, laidback, still handsome and in shape.

KATE WESTMORELAND – 40's. A therapist. Strong-willed, opinionated, smart, sexual and pretty. Great mom, runs her house.

DAYNE WESTMORELAND – 17. A high school senior. This family's golden boy. Confident and very handsome. The best fullback to come out of the state of Mississippi.

GRACIE WESTMORELAND – 15. An overly-dramatic high school sophomore who is consumed with acting and sibling rivalry.

KENDALL PARKER – 15. Effeminate, too pretty to be a boy. Wise beyond his years. He escapes his fundamentalist mother through his love for theatre.

SISTER TIMOTHEA PARKER – 40's. A conservative, crazy religious fundamentalist who abuses her son and justifies it in the name of the Lord.

SETTING

The play takes place in Vicksburg, Mississippi, at the Westmoreland home.

TIME

The play begins in early Fall and ends the following Spring.

For
Greg Julian

In Memory of
Kendall Moore

ACT ONE

Scene One

(The set is a prominent home in Vicksburg, Mississippi. The home is clean, but lived in, somewhat cluttered. The main playing area is a family room/kitchen. A stairway leads to a small landing with two doors on each side. One door is to a teenage boy's bedroom. Another playing area is the front porch outside the home.)

(In darkness, waiters and restaurant customers sing.)

WAITERS & CUSTOMERS. *(voice-over)* "Happy Anniversary, Happy Anniversary, Happy Anniversary, Happy Anniversary!"

(claps, cheers and ad-libs)

(Dayne's bedroom. Lights come up on **DAYNE WESTMORELAND***, a handsome 17-year-old, who is laying out his clothes for school the next day.* **DAYNE** *wears only boxer shorts as he chooses socks, jeans and a football jersey, placing them on a chair. His body is lean and muscular, an obvious athlete. On his wall is a signed poster of a football hero and on the chest-of-drawers are countless football trophies. Dayne's room is much neater than the rest of the house.)*

(Front porch. Laughter is heard, a man's and a woman's, and lights slowly come up as **KATE WESTMORELAND***, 40-ish, and* **BOBBY WESTMORELAND***, also 40-ish, stroll up to the house, hand in hand, a little tipsy. Lights now reflect that a full moon is lighting the happy couple.* **BOBBY** *looks up and points.)*

BOBBY. Look at the moon. It's a full moon.

KATE. You always did love a full moon.

(Dayne's bedroom. **DAYNE** *looks through a drawer, coming up empty.)*

DAYNE. Shit, shit, shit.

(He closes the drawer, then opens another and rummages through it.)

(front porch)

BOBBY. Happy anniversary, baby.

KATE. Happy anniversary. Nineteen years. How did that happen?

BOBBY. Fast. That's how. Too fast. Pretty soon we'll both be dead and we'll wonder why the hell we were so stressed.

KATE. Always the eternal optimist.

*(***BOBBY*** takes* **KATE** *in his arms, kisses her.)*

(Dayne's bedroom. **DAYNE** *gives up, closes the drawer.)*

DAYNE. Shit.

(He exits his room.)

(front porch)

BOBBY. I love you more right now than the day we got married.

KATE. You told me on our wedding day that it was impossible for anyone to love more than you loved me that day.

BOBBY. Well, I was wrong. I've evolved. *(kisses her)* Katie, make me a promise.

KATE. Okay.

BOBBY. Promise me that when I die –

KATE. Oh God, no! Not death talk again. Not on our anniversary! Why do you always go there?

BOBBY. Because I think about it. Ever since Billy was killed in that car wreck, I think about how precious life is. And I worry.

KATE. Well, stop! Billy died over ten years ago. I don't like it when you talk like this. It makes me –

BOBBY. Shh. Just put up with me for one minute. Please.

KATE. Okay, but make it quick. I don't want to dwell on your death on our anniversary. *(sexily)* There are other things I want to dwell on that do not require planning a funeral.

(She reaches down and strokes him.)

BOBBY. *(laughing)* Stop, Miss Horny Toad. Just sit and let me finish what I need to say. Put up with me for a minute.

KATE. *(sighs)* Okay.

(Stairs. DAYNE rushes down the stairs, carrying a load of laundry. He rushes through the kitchen and offstage where we assume he puts his clothes in a washing machine.)

(Porch. BOBBY pulls KATE onto a small bench that sits on the porch, and he stares at the moon.)

BOBBY. If anything ever happens to me…you know that you and the kids are set.

(Living room/kitchen. DAYNE enters from the offstage laundry room, opens the refrigerator. Finding nothing of interest, he closes it, looks in the cabinet, grabs a jar of peanut butter, closes the cabinet, then grabs a banana and spoon and begins eating peanut butter on a banana as he sits on the counter as he studies a football playbook that sits on the bar.)

(front porch)

KATE. *(impatient)* Yes, yes, we'll be millionaires. You're worth more dead to me than you are alive. And the trust portfolio is in the safety deposit box and the key is in your little jewelry box that Gracie made you in Vacation Bible School, where you keep your watches and cuff links.

BOBBY. You are such a smart-ass.

KATE. So, are we done with this conversation?

BOBBY. Just one more thing. It's about the moon.

KATE. The moon?

BOBBY. Yes, the moon. And not just the moon. The full moon. Like that one. You know how I love a full moon.

KATE. Yes, and you also have an unusual fixation with squirrels.

BOBBY. I do. I love those little critters. *(pause)* When I'm gone, I want you to think of me whenever you see a full moon.

KATE. What about squirrels? Do I have to think about you when I see squirrels? Because there are an awful lot of squirrels…Bobby, are you crying?

BOBBY. Maybe a little. I'm mourning my own death, okay?

KATE. You are so silly. *(She wipes his eyes.)* That's what I love about you, Robert Dayne Westmoreland. You're this big ol' handsome lug of a football coach, but when we saw *Terms of Endearment,* you cried like a Mexican widow at a funeral.

BOBBY. That is not politically right, Katie.

KATE. Oh, who cares. *(yells)* Nobody's listening.

BOBBY. Promise me, Katie. Promise you'll think of me whenever you see a full moon. When I'm dead and gone and you look up and see a full moon, promise me you'll think of me.

KATE. Okay. If I happen to look up and see a full moon between my shopping sprees with all that life insurance money, yes, I'll do my utmost best to think of you.

BOBBY. The stores are closed at night, Katie.

KATE. Not during moonlight madness sales. Can we *please* go inside and get naked? I want to do it when I'm still a little tipsy. You know how wild I get when I'm tipsy.

*(She kisses **BOBBY**.)*

BOBBY. Dance with me first.

KATE. Oh dear God in heaven!

*(**BOBBY** gets up and takes **KATE**'s hand.)*

BOBBY. In the moonlight.

KATE. Did you get a prescription for romance pills?

BOBBY. Are you complaining? Because I could be one of those guys that forgets anniversaries and never compliments your hair and only wants to get it on after watching porn on the computer.

KATE. Eeww. Who does that?!

BOBBY. Jesse Carlton does. And every man I know who's been married over five years – except me.

KATE. Well, that's disgusting. I will never be able to look at Jesse Carlton the same way again. Pervert. And poor Rhonda Kaye. Does she know? I was supposed to have lunch with her tomorrow. Oh, I wish you hadn't told me that.

BOBBY. Shhh. Just dance with me. Under the moon, under the stars, then under the sheets.

KATE. No, above the sheets and we'll move the mirror by the bed –

BOBBY. Now you're talkin' –

KATE. *(whispers)* Then I'll… *(She whispers something in his ear.)* …all over my husband's hot naked body.

BOBBY. Damnation! I love it when you talk dirty.

KATE. *(playfully)* So, you still wanna dance?

BOBBY. *(pause, thinks for a moment.)* Just for a moment.

KATE. *(sighs)* We don't have any music.

BOBBY. It'll be in our heads. I'm hearing "Sea of Love".

KATE. Oooh, I like that one.

(They begin to dance.)

BOBBY. I need to work out more. I've lost the six-pack.

KATE. Yeah, but the hard six-plus-one right under where that six-pack once was feels pretty good to me.

BOBBY. Remember that night you measured it?

KATE. You asked me to!

(They laugh.)

You tried so hard to make it seven. So, so close.

(He presses against her.)

BOBBY. I bet it's seven tonight.

(He pushes closer. She strokes him again.)

KATE. Let's go inside, and I'll measure it again.

(She tries to pull him towards the house. He pulls her back into his arms.)

BOBBY. Wait. I want you to remember this night when you see a full moon, us dancing, then making love, a little loving, a little dirty, then falling asleep in each other's arms naked, completely content.

(They make out intensely, **KATE** *throws her leg around* **BOBBY**.*)*

KATE. *(breaking)* Come on! I'm dying here! This is like… like tantric dancing.

(Family room/kitchen. **BOBBY** *and* **KATE** *enter.)*

BOBBY. After you, my dear.

(They laugh and dance some more. **BOBBY** *dips* **KATE**.*)*

DAYNE. Happy anniversary, kids.

*(***KATE** *jumps upon seeing* **DAYNE**, *sitting at the counter.)*

KATE. Jesus, Dayne! You scared me half to death!

BOBBY. I'd stay and talk son, but I might just lose some momentum, if you know what I mean –

DAYNE. *(covers ears)* La, la, la, la, la, la, la. Don't want to hear this. Parents aren't supposed to have sex! Especially as often as y'all do! Go! Go!

BOBBY. And *you* go to bed. It's our big game tomorrow. First game of the season.

DAYNE. I'm ready! We gonna kick some Cougar ass!

KATE. Come on!

*(***KATE** *and* **BOBBY** *laugh and exit.* **DAYNE** *turns off the light in the kitchen and heads up the stairs.)*

DAYNE. *(calling)* Mom, will you put my clothes in the dryer when you get up in the morning? I need my lucky boxers.

KATE. *(offstage)* Yes…

(blackout)

(during blackout)

MRS. LANE. *(voice-over)* Your audition will consist of a one minute monologue and a song of your choice. And I do *not* want you to do any songs or monologues from *Oklahoma.*

GRACIE. *(voice-over, whispers)* This is retarded.

MRS. LANE. *(voice-over)* Gracie Westmoreland, if you have something to say, say it to the entire class.

GRACIE. *(voice-over)* Oh…Well, Kendall and I were wondering…Mrs. Lane, why is that? That we can't do something from the musical we're auditioning for? We don't understand.

MRS. LANE. *(voice-over)* It's my way of directing. I like to see the acting and singing ability outside the play we're doing.

KENDALL. *(voice-over, whispers, sarcastic)* Oh, that makes so much sense.

MRS. LANE. *(voice-over)* Did you say something, Kendall Parker?

Scene Two

(It's the next morning before work and school.)

(Family room/kitchen. **KATE**, *professionally dressed, makes breakfast while talking on a cordless phone.)*

(Dayne's bedroom. **DAYNE**, *in his bed, is still asleep.)*

(Family room/kitchen. **GRACIE WESTMORELAND**, *a dramatic 15-year-old, sits at the piano, pecking out a melody and singing.)*

GRACIE. "There's a place I sometimes go... there is a place...place...I sometimes go..."

(She continues.)

KATE. *(on phone)* Al, Al, Al! You have to stop crying because I can only understand about half of what you are saying. *(covers receiver)* Gracie. Gracie! Could you hold off on that for just one moment and go make sure your brother is awake.

GRACIE. *(attitude)* Oh, of course. Because my career is not important to this family at all –

KATE. You're in high school, you don't have a career. Now go wake up your brother. *(back in phone)* Al, Al...AL! –

GRACIE. I hate my existence.

*(**GRACIE** starts up the stairs, pauses at the mirror on the landing to primp.)*

KATE. Our session is in less than two hours. Compose yourself and don't do anything drastic, promise me.

(She goes to the front door, opens it, grabs the newspaper and sets it on the bar.)

(Dayne's room. **GRACIE** *slams Dayne's door, hard!* **DAYNE** *stirs, doesn't wake up.)*

Yes, yes, I know she's cheated on you before, but that doesn't mean... Well, I'm sure she has a logical explanation for that. Al! Put down the gun, you're a democrat. I really have to go now! I'll see you at nine.

(**KATE** *hangs up and pours orange juice into glasses.* **BOBBY** *enters, wearing a blue polo/coach shirt, khaki pants and a baseball hat.*)

BOBBY. Today's the day! First game of the season. Our son's senior year. And it's…it's gonna be a good one.

(He kisses **KATE**, *then picks up the newspaper sitting on the bar, settles at the table.)*

KATE. I'm feeling state champions third year in a row.

(Dayne's bedroom. **GRACIE** *enters, looks around disgusted.)*

GRACIE. God, I hate perfection.

(She rearranges some of Dayne's trophies, smiles, then takes his neatly laid out clothes and throws them on the floor.)

(family room/kitchen)

BOBBY. Who was that? On the phone?

(**KATE** *brings* **BOBBY** *some bacon and eggs. She sets the plate on the table, then takes off his hat, puts it on the table.*)

KATE. A patient. It's just too early to deal with suicide threats, which are not valid. I hope. Hmmm, you smell good.

BOBBY. It's that Hugo stuff you got me.

KATE. Boss. Hugo Boss. I have very good taste.

BOBBY. You married me, didn't you?

(Dayne's bedroom. **GRACIE** *goes over and pushes* **DAYNE**, *hard.)*

GRACIE. Get up!

(**DAYNE** *grunts, stirs.* **GRACIE** *exits.*)

(family room/kitchen)

KATE. You were a crazy man last night.

BOBBY. I was inspired.

(Dayne's bedroom/landing/stairs. As **GRACIE** *pauses and primps again,* **DAYNE** *jumps up, looks at alarm.)*

DAYNE. Shit!!! *(yells)* Why didn't someone wake me up?!

GRACIE. *(yells back)* I just did, genius! And you're welcome!

*(***DAYNE*** notices the out-of-place trophies.)*

DAYNE. *(mutters)* Little bitch. *(yells)* Mom, tell Gracie to leave my stuff alone!

(He puts them back the way they were, then sees the jeans, picks them up.)

(Family room/kitchen. **GRACIE** *enters.)*

KATE. What did you do?

GRACIE. Nothing.

KATE. You know how I feel about lying.

GRACIE. Yes, *(quoting)* "lying and violence are the two things I will not tolerate young lady."

*(***GRACIE*** goes back to the piano as* **KATE** *hands* **BOBBY** *a plate of biscuits as he begins to read the sports section.)*

BOBBY. *(to* **GRACIE.***)* Hey, angel face. You good this morning?

GRACIE. No!

KATE. *(to* **BOBBY***)* And why would today be different from every other day.

BOBBY. Well, you hang in there, Gracie. Before you die, you might just have one good day yet. Something to look forward to.

GRACIE. Not funny, Dad!

KATE. Gracie, come eat your breakfast before it gets cold. *(yelling)* Dayne! Breakfast!

(Dayne's bedroom)

DAYNE. I'll be right down after I shower.

(He then exits to an offstage bathroom. There is a knock at the front door.)

(family room/kitchen)

GRACIE. I'll get it. It's Kendall. *(back to* **KATE***)* And I'm not eating. I have to lose five pounds by my audition – thanks to you and your gene pool. *(answers door, overly dramatic)* Hey, Kendall. I am in so much trouble. I can't find the right song to sing for the audition and I'm fat.

*(***KENDALL PARKER** *enters. He's 15, effeminate, too pretty for a boy,* **GRACIE***'s best friend.)*

KENDALL. Well, I don't know what monologue to do, but with my song I'm going to take a risk and please don't judge me because I've made up my mind. Are you ready? I'm singing "On My Own" from *Les Mis*.

GRACIE. Isn't that a – ?

KENDALL. I know, I know, it's a girl's song, sung by Eponine just longing to be with Marius and eaten up with jealousy of Cosette. The given circumstances are so complicated…I can go so deep…not being able to be with the man you love and living through fantasy. So sad.

GRACIE. Please don't cry! The auditions aren't 'til this afternoon.

KENDALL. I'm not! Oh, and it's perfect for my range. I'm changing all references to the genders and singing it really, well…manly. But who can do a monologue in just one minute? It's just unreasonable!

GRACIE. I know! I'm freaking out, Kendall!

KENDALL. And why do they always choose those tired old musicals? *Oklahoma?* Please! Why not *Nine* or *Chicago?*

BOBBY. Mornin', Kendall.

KENDALL. Hello, Coach Westmoreland. *(to* **GRACIE***)* I guess Vicksburg, Mississippi is just too conservative for *Nine* and *Chicago*. And they would never do *Kiss of The Spider Woman!* I could tear up Molina. I hope I have a shot at Curly but I'd be happy with Will. I do not want Judd!

GRACIE. I don't think you have to worry.

BOBBY. Gracie, angel face, you look beautiful the way you are. You don't want to be one of those anorexic looking models who –

GRACIE. Oh, yes I do! And if you had been kind enough to pass me your genes instead of just to Dayne, then I wouldn't have the Fuller women thunder-thigh problem.

BOBBY. *(to KATE)* Like I had a choice.

KATE. So now I have thunder thighs?

BOBBY. No, you don't.

GRACIE. Yes, you do! *(back to KENDALL)* I thought you were going to do the closing argument from *To Kill A Mockingbird*?

KENDALL. Too long! Can't figure out what to cut. And it's just too important to damage. In my opinion, one of the most perfect literary pieces ever written. It would be sacrilegious to cut one single word!

GRACIE. I don't get why we can't do a song from *Oklahoma*? I just don't know what to choose! Those stupid audition rules! Although "Surrey With The Fringe On Top" is so retarded. What the hell is a "surrey" anyway?

KENDALL. A carriage. A horse-drawn carriage. And I don't mean to be harsh, but Mrs. Lane is just not a director. She doesn't understand an actor's process.

GRACIE. I know! Old school. *(sing-song)* Those who can't, teach.

KATE. Morning, Kendall.

KENDALL. Good morning.

KATE. Would you like to have some breakfast? There's plenty since Gracie isn't eating, and I probably shouldn't with my massive thunder thighs.

KENDALL. No, ma'am, I'm just a bundle of nerves and would just throw up all over the place if I ate anything. But thank you.

KATE. Well, that's very considerate of you. You are the best singer in the whole school, Kendall, so I don't think you'll have a problem getting cast.

KENDALL. Thank you.

*(He heads over to the bar and sits to talk to **KATE**. **GRACIE** continues to study her song, half listening.)*

KATE. How's your mother? Does she know you're auditioning this year?

KENDALL. Oh God no! Mrs. Lane knows my situation and already told me that if I got cast, she wouldn't schedule anything on Wednesday night so I won't miss prayer meeting. And no shows or rehearsals on Sundays. I've told my mother that I joined the Math Club and the Science Club and the Spanish Club and now that I'm in student government as Drama Club representative, it'll be easy to make up after school meetings and not get caught.

GRACIE. Well, at least I don't have religious fanatics for parents.

KENDALL. Parent. Just one. Thank God!

KATE. I wish your mother could see how wonderful you are.

(family room/kitchen)

KENDALL. Well, she sees me sing at church and I had a great solo in the Christmas cantata. Remember?

GRACIE. Yeah, great.

KENDALL. That's enough for her. *(imitating)* "Theatre is the devil's playground." Well, that and movies and television and rap music and even Celine Dion! Trust me, it's better to just not tell her. She's so clueless about anything but the church that –

*(**DAYNE** rushes down the stairs, in warm-ups, wet hair, no shirt. He goes to the bar, chest at **KENDALL**'s eye level. **KENDALL** completely loses focus, stops talking and stares as **KATE** hands **DAYNE** a glass of orange juice.)*

DAYNE. I need my lucky boxers –

KATE. Oh crap. Honey, I forgot to dry them.

DAYNE. Mom! Granddaddy Fuller gave me those for luck! You know I have to wear them on game days.

GRACIE. *(to* **KENDALL***)* Close your mouth, Kendall, and help me with my song.

*(***KENDALL** *obeys, then heads to the piano as* **DAYNE** *sits at the table by* **BOBBY.***)*

KATE. Honey, I'm sorry, I was dealing with a patient.

DAYNE. Thanks a lot.

BOBBY. Hey! Give your mom a break. She does important things. Maybe prevented a suicide. How often can you say you've done that, huh? *(slugs* **DAYNE***)* Just throw them in the dryer. They'll be dry in less than ten minutes.

KATE. I'll do it. Eat some breakfast, sweetie.

*(***KATE** *exits.* **DAYNE** *grabs a couple of biscuits, fills them with bacon and starts eating.* **KENDALL** *keeps glancing over at* **DAYNE** *as he sits at the piano and thumbs through a songbook with* **GRACIE.***)*

BOBBY. You excited?

DAYNE. *(gobbling bites)* Yep. I'm running so late. I don't know what's wrong with me. I can't wake up in the mornings and I stay too tired. I hope it doesn't affect my game.

BOBBY. You stay up too late. You're probably still on summer time. Got to hit the hay earlier. You sure looked good in practice this week. Better than ever.

*(***KATE** *enters, carrying an Ole Miss sleeveless T-shirt.*)

KATE. All done. Here, put this on. *(hands him the T-shirt)* I'm sorry I forgot, Dayne. Do you want some eggs?

DAYNE. Uh-huh. It's okay. Sorry I was pissy.

*(***DAYNE** *puts the shirt down.*)

KATE. Uh-uh. You know you don't sit at the table without a shirt.

*(***DAYNE** *puts on the shirt.*)

DAYNE. *(mutters)* Stupid rule.

*(***BOBBY** *smiles and nods, picks up his hat to show* **DAYNE***, agreeing.*)

DAYNE. Will you pick me up some vitamins today, Mom? I need more energy. And my weight-gain powder. I lost more weight.

KATE. *(whispers)* Well, don't tell Gracie.

BOBBY. It's because of all the practice. Lean, mean fighting machine.

KATE. I'll stop by the Vitamin Shack.

(KATE scrambles some eggs. KENDALL starts playing piano and GRACIE starts to sing.)

GRACIE. *(singing)* "There is a place, I sometimes go –"

DAYNE. *(mock look around)* Do I hear cats fighting?

GRACIE. I heard that! *(bursting into tears)* I'm insecure enough about my singing as it is, asshole!

BOBBY. Hey, potty mouth!

GRACIE. Yeah, go ahead and take his side like you always do! Dayne can never do anything wrong –

DAYNE. I was just kidding.

GRACIE. I hate you!

KATE. *(overlapping)* Say you're sorry. Hurry!

GRACIE. Well, it's my day too!

DAYNE. *(overlapping)* Sorry, jeez –

GRACIE. Just because it's the first game of the stupid season doesn't mean I don't have a life too! I get so tired of you and football. Nobody supports the arts –

KENDALL. I do –

KATE. Honey, we love your acting.

(KATE serves DAYNE his eggs. DAYNE gets up, opens the refrigerator and pours himself some milk.)

GRACIE. But I'm not a good singer! Just say it! Dayne already did! I have to audition today and I have to sing. You don't know what it's like. It'd be like Meryl Streep's husband telling her that her accent wasn't right when she auditioned for *Out of Africa* or *Cry In The Dark* or *Sophie's Choice* –

DAYNE. Here we go with Meryl freakin' Streep –

(**DAYNE** *sits and eats his breakfast.*)

KENDALL. I don't think Meryl Streep has to audition.

GRACIE. Oh shut up, Kendall! That's not the point. *(turns on* **DAYNE***)* And don't call her "Meryl freakin' Streep"! She happens to be the best actress that ever walked the face of the earth and you just said I couldn't sing and I wasn't going to get cast in the Fall musical again. *(bangs table)* Dayne! Just because you already have scholarship offers, UNDER THE TABLE, illegal recruiting –

BOBBY. Hey, don't talk about that – !

KATE. Okay, this is getting absurd –

BOBBY. You can't talk about that, Gracie.

GRACIE. Well, since you're a therapist, make it better, *Mother!* And you never missed one of Dayne's games and you missed my performance in *A Fairy Tale Review.*

KATE. When you were in sixth grade! I had the Hong Kong flu! I was in bed with a hundred and three temperature!

GRACIE. Whatever.

BOBBY. And I was there.

DAYNE. So was I. You were riveting as "Little Red Riding Hood".

GRACIE. Shut up, Dayne! This has nothing to do with you!

DAYNE. Oh, I thought it did. I thought it was called sibling rivalry. That you are jealous 'cause –

GRACIE. And it's not fair that you got Dad's gene pool and I got Mom's thunder thighs –

KATE. My thighs are not thunderous!

BOBBY. Okay, stop it! We're very supportive of your acting and you know it –

(**DAYNE** *gets up, rinses his plate, glass, and silverware and puts them in the dishwasher.*)

KENDALL. I just think you're feeling insecure about your singing –

GRACIE. No shit, genius!

BOBBY. Hey, potty mouth – !

DAYNE. I'm out of here. Yell at me when my lucky boxers are dry.

KATE. Did you get enough breakfast? It's game day and –

GRACIE. Great! Back to Dayne. It's all about Dayne!

*(**KENDALL** stares as **DAYNE** passes by. **DAYNE** gives him a mock punch and smiles.)*

DAYNE. Good luck with your audition, Ken. And try and get Hysterical Hannah to calm down –

GRACIE. SHUT UP! SHUT UP! SHUT UP! I AM NOT HYSTERICAL!!! *(to **KENDALL**)* And quit staring at him all the time, Kendall! You're just proving my point that he got all the good genes and I got Mom's thunder-thighs and nobody can sing in this family and I am so screwed –

BOBBY. Okay, stop it, Grace Louise. Now! Enough!

GRACIE. *(screaming)* AHHHHH! You know I hate my middle name, so don't call me Grandmother Fuller with the big ol' thunder thighs name!

BOBBY. Okay, I'm sorry. But just calm down and sit down for a moment.

GRACIE. No!

BOBBY. Now!

*(Dayne's bedroom. **DAYNE** enters, picks up his football playbook, studies it.)*

*(Family room/kitchen. **GRACIE** sits, arms crossed.)*

GRACIE. Okay, *what?*

BOBBY. Angel face, we love you so much and we are so proud of you. You are a brilliant actress –

GRACIE. I know that!

KATE. You're going to be the next Meryl Streep.

GRACIE. *(crying)* But Meryl can sing.

BOBBY. She can?

GRACIE. Hello?! *Postcards From The Edge, A Prairie Home Companion* –

KENDALL. *Mama Mia.*

GRACIE. Meryl's got it all and I don't.

KATE. There are lots of other actresses, sweetie, Academy Award winners, who cannot sing. Kate Winslet. Cher. And Meryl has a good voice, but it's not great –

GRACIE. But I want to be in the musical! Acting is my life and if I don't get cast, I'll just die. What'll I do all Fall? Watch Dayne make touchdowns? Kendall's right. I'm just insecure about my singing and I've worked so hard, but Molly Miller's going to get "Laurie," I just know it. I can act circles around that little bitch –

BOBBY. Hey – !

GRACIE. …but she has that voice and musical theatre is *not* known for good acting. And why did the auditions have to be on the same day as Dayne's first game? He's gonna be the superstar and win and I'm not going to get cast again! I hate musicals! They're stupid and unrealistic!

KENDALL. I don't think you should even audition for "Laurie". Audition for "Ado Annie", then you can sing in a character voice.

GRACIE. I am *not* a character actress! I am a leading lady! And who the hell breaks into song in real life anyway?

KENDALL. I sometimes do –

GRACIE. Of course you do!

KATE. Don't be mean to Kendall. He's just trying to help –

GRACIE. Is it your mission in life, *Mother*, to take everybody's side except mine?!! I hate my existence!

(She storms up the stairs.)

KATE. Where did she come from?

BOBBY. Your gene pool.

(lights begin to fade)

*(Dayne's bedroom. **DAYNE** puts the book down, rises.)*

DAYNE. *(yelling)* Mom! Are my lucky boxers dry yet?

(blackout)

(during blackout)

(crowd cheers throughout)

FOOTBALL ANNOUNCER. *(voice-over)* Westmoreland to the twenty-five! To the twenty! He's got daylight! One man to beat! Oh what a move! To the ten... five. Touchdown!!! Touchdown Bobcats! Dayne Westmoreland racks up another huge gain on a thirty-two yard scamper for the touchdown as the Bobcats go up thirteen, zero! *(pause)* Short screen to Westmoreland on the right side. Look out, he's got blockers out front. He's to midfield...to the forty... the thirty...nobody is going to touch him! And Dayne Westmoreland walks into the end zone for the fourth time tonight as the Bobcats go up twenty-seven, zero! *(pause)* And that folks is what you call an old-fashioned blowout! Final score, Vicksburg Prep Bobcats, twenty-eight, Yazoo City Trojans, a big fat zero!

Scene Three

*(Fornt porch. **TIMOTHEA PARKER**, 40, high, 1970's Pentecostal hair, no make-up or jewelry, sits on the bench outside the front door of the Westmoreland home. Her dress is conservative, four inches below the knee. She is clutching a white Bible tightly, praying. She is very troubled and is crying softly.)*

TIMOTHEA. I know there are demons in this world, Lord, and if my boy is possessed, I ask that you send an angel or your Son, our Lord and Savior Jesus Christ, to exorcise that demon from him so he will walk with thee, dear Lord. *(quoting)* "And Jesus rebuked the demon and he departed out of him, and the child was cured from that very hour." Matthew 17:18. I gave him a test and he failed just like when Christ did to Peter who betrayed him three times before the cock crowed. I want to be a good Mother. I want to raise my boy in thy light, dear sweet precious Savior, to be a God-fearing disciple of thine, but I have failed. *(crying)* I have failed! And I need you to help me get this child of mine on your spiritual path to Glory –

(A car approaches and headlights hit the house.)

In thy precious holy name, Amen. *(squints; yells)* Matthew Mark! Matthew Mark!

(A car door slams.)

KATE. *(offstage)* Timothea?

*(**KATE** enters, carrying two bags of groceries and never puts them down during her conversation with **TIMOTHEA**.)*

Is everything okay?

TIMOTHEA. This world is exactly as it should be, Kate Westmoreland, because our Lord and Savior is in command –

KATE. I assume you're looking for Kendall.

TIMOTHEA. Please do not utter his secular name in my presence. The boy's name is Matthew Mark. Biblical name. Disciples of our Lord and Master. And by him taking that secular name, he has defied me and his Lord –

KATE. Okay, Ken…Matthew Mark went with us to the football game –

TIMOTHEA. As I suspected. Sinful sport –

KATE. It was over about thirty minutes ago. Bobby is bringing them home. He'll be here shortly. Vicksburg won.

TIMOTHEA. I do not care, Kate Westmoreland –

KATE. Kate is more than adequate. And why don't you give the boy a little breathing room. He's such a good kid.

TIMOTHEA. Uh, uh, uh. Do not tell me how to mother my child, Kate Westmoreland. *(emotional)* He's all I have left. After I lost his twin. And his worthless daddy left us for that…woman.

KATE. Okay, I'm sorry I brought it up. I know that's painful for you.

TIMOTHEA. Oh, I pray for you daily, Kate Westmoreland. I pray that the Father will reach down into the depths of your soul. So you will get off that broad and winding road that leads to destruction –

KATE. Look, I've told you before, I don't want to discuss religion with you. It's a no-win situation.

TIMOTHEA. Oh, I've already won, Kate Westmoreland. My mansion is already built –

KATE. *(can't resist)* Why do you people always have to have such luxury in heaven? Streets of gold. Mansions? Seems a little materialistic to me.

TIMOTHEA. Oh, like the great gospel songwriter-singer Dottie Rambo wrote, "Build my mansion next door to Jesus and tell the angels I'm coming soon!" The Lord wants the very best for those who have accepted him as their personal Savior. And he has a place for you. He has a mansion for you! There is room. Don't you want that? You are a sinner, Kate Westmoreland, and he is giving you free will. You have set your children on a path of destruction and your soul is in grave danger –

KATE. Like I said, *I am done!* And if I don't get to tell you how to mother your child, don't you dare tell me how to mother mine.

TIMOTHEA. Will you sit and pray with me, invite Jesus into your heart?

KATE. No! We're Episcopalians –

TIMOTHEA. Catholics light –

KATE. *(can't resist)* Okay, I'm sorry, but you really think you deserve that real estate next door to Jesus? Over, oh say, Mother Theresa? Ghandi? Billy Graham – ?

TIMOTHEA. *(laughs, amused)* Buddists do not go to heaven. Ghandi is in hell. With Mother Theresa most likely. Catholics are not real Christians with their idolatry, their statues and praying to Mary, a mere mortal –

(A car approaches, headlights hit the house.)

KATE. Thank God –

TIMOTHEA. *(squints)* Matthew! Matthew Mark!

KATE. Ghandi was Hindu.

*(**TIMOTHEA** turns, gives **KATE** a questioning look.)*

TIMOTHEA. I don't think so.

*(**KENDALL** and **GRACIE** enter, followed by **BOBBY**.)*

Why must you defy me, Matthew Mark?

KENDALL. Mother! I told you I'd be home after the game –

BOBBY. Evening, Mrs. Parker.

TIMOTHEA. Hello, Bobby Westmoreland. And I'd appreciate you calling me Sister Timothea. I am no longer married to that man who betrayed the sanctity of our vows. I am now married to Jesus.

BOBBY. Well, that conjures up images that I'm not real comfortable with. Gracie, come on.

*(**BOBBY** and **GRACIE** walk into the house, they both head to offstage bedrooms to change.)*

TIMOTHEA. *(glares at* **BOBBY**, *then to* **KENDALL***)* And I told you to choose between a secular football game and visitation with the elderly and afflicted at the Fairhaven Nursing Home, where you would have brought one ounce of joy into those pitiful, sad, lives by singing hymns with the beautiful voice the Lord bestowed upon you, but instead –

KENDALL. You said I had a choice – !

TIMOTHEA. And I expected you to make the right one!

KENDALL. Then that's not a choice! I don't like singing for those old people. It smells there.

TIMOTHEA. "Children obey your parents in the Lord; for this is right." Ephesians 6:1.

(off **KENDALL** *rolling his eyes)*

You are corrupted, Matthew Mark. Your Father corrupted you before he left with that Jezebel – and this family – these Episcopalians – are corrupting my one and only child. *(emotional)* I'm losing you, Matthew Mark –

KENDALL. I want to be called Kendall!

TIMOTHEA. *(flinches)* I will not utter that name. That is the name of the demon inside of you –

KATE. Oh for crying out loud! I think you need to leave.

TIMOTHEA. Yes, I shall and I will!

KENDALL. *(to* **KATE***)* Sorry. *(to* **TIMOTHEA***)* Let's just go! Jeez!

TIMOTHEA. Do *not* use the Lord's name in vain. That word is a slang word for Jesus Christ, our Lord, Master, and Savior!

KENDALL. You're embarrassing me!

*(***KENDALL** *stalks off the porch,* **TIMOTHEA** *follows.)*

TIMOTHEA. You let me down, Matthew Mark. But most of all, you let down the Lord and all of His creations who are knocking on death's door –

(Family room/kitchen. **KATE** *enters the house, goes to the kitchen and puts up the groceries.* **BOBBY** *comes from the*

bedroom to help with the groceries, **GRACIE** *comes down the stairs.)*

KATE. That poor, poor boy –

GRACIE. She scares me. She speaks in tongues, you know?

KATE. Yes. Pentecostals.

GRACIE. When I went to their church that time, she did it in the middle of the Christmas Cantata. Scary.

(**GRACIE** *pulls out her cell phone, looks at a text, then starts text messaging back and continues all throughout the scene.)*

KATE. I know.

GRACIE. She made a shepherd cry.

KATE. Now could you stop for one moment and be thankful for your parents.

GRACIE. No. Because there are parents who are better than you.

KATE. Of course. She actually said that Ghandi and Mother Theresa are in hell.

BOBBY. Sorry I missed that conversation. Hey, how about that game!?

KATE. It was a great game, Bobby.

GRACIE. It was good. I've seen better.

KATE. Gracie, you want ice cream? Now that your audition is over.

GRACIE. No! If I get "Laurie," I don't want to have to take off the five pounds you are trying to put on me to make yourself feel better about your own obesity.

(She rolls her eyes, then texts messages with fervor.)

KATE. Now I'm obese?

BOBBY. You're not obese, Katie. Well, I want ice cream. Time to celebrate. You want some?

(**BOBBY** *scoops a bowl of ice cream.)*

KATE. Not with these thighs.

BOBBY. And that was a great game, Gracie. There are levels of great. When your team wins by twenty-eight points and the other team doesn't score, that's a great game.

(**BOBBY** *settles on the couch.* **GRACIE** *flutters around, unsettled. She checks her cell phone to make sure it is on. She begins to text.*)

KATE. Was Dayne going out with his friends? I got him some vitamins and his weight-gain powder.

BOBBY. I think so. *(back to* **GRACIE***)* Which were mostly scored by your brother, young lady.

GRACIE. *(as she texts)* Yes, it's all about Dayne again. Thanks for asking about my audition.

KATE. I asked you twice about your audition and you said you didn't want to talk about it.

GRACIE. I don't!

BOBBY. Well, I want to know. How was your audition, angel face?

GRACIE. I said I don't want to talk about it! Can't you respect that, Dad? I never get any support from this family!

(She rushes upstairs. **BOBBY** *starts to get up.)*

KATE. Don't! Sit down and let her go pout. It'll at least give us a moment of peace.

BOBBY. We just can't win.

KATE. I've stopped trying. And you really need to reevaluate that pet name "angel face". It no longer applies. Well, come to think of it, it never did. It was a great game, honey.

BOBBY. Yes ma'am, it was.

(They kiss as the sound of another car approaches and headlights hit the house.)

There's Dayne. Promise we can celebrate later?

KATE. Two nights in a row? I don't know if you can handle it.

*(Front porch. **DAYNE** approaches the house. He pauses, closes his eyes, leans against the house, and takes a deep breath. Then another.)*

BOBBY. Oh, I can handle it. The question is, Katie, can you handle it?

KATE. Like you have *ever* been able to keep up with me.

BOBBY. Well, that is true.

*(**GRACIE** appears at the top of the stairs.)*

GRACIE. I'm going to bed! Good night!

(She storms off, slams door.)

KATE. *(sarcastic)* Sweet dreams.

*(**DAYNE** enters the living room.)*

BOBBY. There's our star! You were spectacular tonight, son.

DAYNE. *(no enthusiasm)* Yeah, it was a great game.

KATE. What's wrong?

DAYNE. I don't know. Just kinda exhausted. The guys and them went over to D.J.'s to hang, but, I don't know, I just feel like going to bed.

BOBBY. Hey, you left it all on the field. Four touchdowns. I was good, but never that good.

DAYNE. Come on, Dad, you played pro.

BOBBY. Barely.

DAYNE. I do love that game. And you blew out your knee, Dad. Not fair.

KATE. You want something to eat? There's leftover roast. How about a roast beef sandwich?

DAYNE. I'm not hungry, but I guess I should eat.

BOBBY. Refill? Game wore me out too.

*(**BOBBY** hands his empty ice cream bowl to **KATE**.)*

DAYNE. I've been thinking, Dad. I want to play pro, but what do you do after? Don't you need a backup?

KATE. Yes! And you're smart, so yes, think of a backup.

*(**KATE** refills **BOBBY**'s ice cream bowl.)*

BOBBY. Unlike your old man, who can only coach and teach P.E. But see, I was smarter than most folks gave me credit for. I married the smartest girl in town. My sugar mama. *That* was my backup plan.

KATE. You could have done something else.

(**KATE** *hands the ice cream bowl to* **DAYNE.**)

You didn't want to. Hand this to your daddy.

(**DAYNE** *passes the ice cream to* **BOBBY** *as* **KATE** *proceeds to make* **DAYNE**'s *sandwich.*)

BOBBY. Nope. I'm too stupid to do anything else.

KATE. Don't listen to your dad. He was smart enough. He didn't apply himself. He was a typical jock who had no other interests or plans. You do.

BOBBY. We can't all be like you, Katie.

KATE. That's not what I was saying –

BOBBY. I know you wish I was more than just a high school football coach.

KATE. "Were" more. Subjunctive tense. You love what you do. I love that you love what you do and I'm not having this discussion again.

BOBBY. Then why do you always bring it up?

KATE. I didn't bring it up. Dayne brought it up.

BOBBY. And you ran with it.

DAYNE. Kids, kids! You're a great coach, Dad, and Mom, you're pretty.

KATE. And you're smart, don't you forget it.

DAYNE. I wouldn't be, you know…do this…be so good… it's because…if it weren't for you. I'm glad he's a coach, Mom. My coach. *(smiles to* **BOBBY***, slugs his arm)* Coach Westmoreland.

KATE. *(She's not.)* Yeah. Me too.

BOBBY. Uh-huh. Well son, coaching you has been the highlight of my career. More than playing that one year for the Broncos. Just watching you… *(chokes up)* …guiding you…you're just so damn good.

DAYNE. Dad, are you about to cry?

BOBBY. No. No. Of course not.

(**KATE** *takes sandwich, hands it to* **DAYNE**, *then sits behind* **BOBBY** *on the arm of the couch.*)

KATE. Yes he is. You know your dad. And it's healthy. Men should allow themselves to cry.

BOBBY. Here comes our therapy session.

KATE. Our society…especially in the South…Southern men…well, it's just ridiculous. *(puts her arms around* **BOBBY***'s neck)* And I love that about you.

BOBBY. But you wish I was…*were* more than a football coach.

(**KATE** *grabs* **BOBBY***'s ice cream and moves to the chair, miffed.*)

KATE. We've moved on, Bobby, so drop it. *(to* **DAYNE***)* Oh, I got your vitamins and powder. Right there on the counter.

(She points.)

(**DAYNE** *bites into the sandwich.*)

DAYNE. *(mouth full)* Thanks, maybe they'll give me energy. Good sandwich, Mom. I fell asleep today in history class.

BOBBY. That's called boredom.

KATE. I loved history!

DAYNE. I wasn't bored –

BOBBY. You loved every subject, Katie. I hated it. Too much about the past.

KATE. *(to* **DAYNE***)* Your daddy is a silly, silly man.

DAYNE. I just couldn't hold my eyes open. I feel like something's wrong with me. Maybe I'm coming down with something.

(**KATE** *feels his forehead.*)

Mr. Landrum banged my desk and woke me up. He was pissed.

KATE. You are as cool as a cucumber.

(She sits at the table by **DAYNE**.*)*

Honey, sometimes I think, well, psychologically, that maybe you've gotten into the habit of expecting to be sick.

BOBBY. Interesting –

DAYNE. But I haven't had any, you know, those issues in a long time. I only missed five days of school last year.

BOBBY. You gonna eat the rest of that sandwich?

DAYNE. No. All yours.

*(***BOBBY** *finishes* **DAYNE***'s sandwich.)*

KATE. You're so much better. Remember, Dr. McDonough said he thought that that…issue…was behind you.

BOBBY. No pun intended.

DAYNE. Shut up, Dad!

BOBBY. You know, I.B.S. Irritable bowel syndrome – behind you –

DAYNE. We get it, Dad! Not funny.

BOBBY. Sorry, couldn't resist. And Jerry Landrum is a brainiac who hates the sports department. He didn't have to bang your desk. On game day? He's a closet case. Bottled up anger. Your Uncle Greg proved that you don't have to stay in the closet.

KATE. Your brother moved to New York and works in advertising and design.

DAYNE. Still ain't easy being gay in Vicksburg, Mississippi.

KATE. "Not." It's "not" easy.

BOBBY. Then Jerry Landrum should move to a big city like your uncle. Atlanta maybe.

DAYNE. He's actually a really good teacher. I shouldn't have fallen asleep in his class.

(The phone rings. **KATE** *answers it.)*

KATE. I got it.

BOBBY. *(thinking)* He sits alone eating his sack lunch in the teacher's lounge every day. Maybe I'll join him tomorrow –

KATE. *(in phone)* Hello. Oh, hello Mrs. Lane. I hope this is good news. Because I couldn't take it otherwise. She's been in a mood.

BOBBY. You know, reach out.

KATE. Did you try her cell?

BOBBY. I don't want him to think I'm like other people. Wonder if he knows about Greg? Maybe I'll tell him.

KATE. *(in phone)* Oh this is great. No, no. I'll let you tell her. Hold on. *(covers receiver)* Gracie! Telephone!

BOBBY. Hey, Dayne, always look out for Kendall. Like I did for your Uncle Greg, okay?

DAYNE. I already do that.

KATE. *(calling)* Gracie!

BOBBY. Good man.

(GRACIE appears at the top of the stairs.)

GRACIE. Who is it?

KATE. Mrs. Lane. Why didn't you answer your cell?

(GRACIE bounds down the stairs and KATE hands her the phone.)

GRACIE. *(nervous rant)* I turned it off because I knew they were going to make the calls tonight and I knew I probably wouldn't be cast, so I knew it wouldn't ring, but then there was like still that slight possibility I would get cast…and everybody would text me that they got cast…or didn't…and I don't want to do props again…so I eliminated the possibility of getting a call because I was just so nervous and I was wishing I could talk to Meryl Streep…if she ever wasn't cast…or they made her do props…or lights…and maybe I would get a call anyway…out of pity or to do props or something retarded like every other year. And people would text me, you know?

BOBBY. Did anybody follow that?

DAYNE. Hell, no –

GRACIE. Shut up, Dayne. You don't understand rejection.

KATE. Honey, just talk to her.

GRACIE. *(realizing she's holding the phone)* Oh. *(in phone, nervous)* Hello –

(She settles on the piano bench as she talks. **DAYNE** *gets up and puts his plate in the sink, passing* **KATE**. **KATE** *stares at* **DAYNE**, *suddenly expresses concern.)*

GRACIE. Hi, Mrs. Lane.

KATE. Dayne, come back here –

DAYNE. What?

GRACIE. I did? I got cast?!

BOBBY. That's great angel face.

GRACIE. *(listens, then disappointed)* Oh, okay.

KATE. Come back here in the light.

GRACIE. What about Kendall?

*(**DAYNE** stands in front of **KATE**.)*

DAYNE. What's up?

GRACIE. *(trying to be enthusiastic)* Oh, good. He'll be a good "Will Parker".

*(**KATE** looks at **DAYNE** closely, now very concerned.)*

KATE. Bobby.

BOBBY. What?

GRACIE. Well, thank you, Mrs. Lane.

KATE. Bobby, come here.

GRACIE. *(holding back tears)* No, I'm really happy. Goodbye.

BOBBY. *(to **KATE**)* What is it?

*(**GRACIE** hangs up and bursts into tears as **BOBBY** heads over to **DAYNE**.)*

GRACIE. She fucking cast me as "Aunt Eller"!

BOBBY. Hey, hey, hey! Watch it, potty mouth.

GRACIE. I didn't even audition for that old bag!

KATE. Bobby, he's yellow –

BOBBY. What?

DAYNE. What do you mean "yellow"?

GRACIE. Does anybody care that my life just ended?!

KATE. Gracie, hush!

  *(**GRACIE** runs up the stairs.)*

KATE. *(panics)* Bobby, look at his eyes. They're yellow.

DAYNE. Yellow?

  *(She looks closer at **DAYNE**'s skin.)*

KATE. He's yellow.

  *(**BOBBY** sees it now.)*

BOBBY. Oh…God –

  (blackout)

  (during blackout)

DOCTOR. *(voice-over)* We've tested him for hepatitis, cirrhosis of the liver, HIV. Negative on all counts.

BOBBY. *(voice-over)* Then what is it? Doc, what's wrong with my boy?

DOCTOR. *(voice-over)* I'm sorry. We don't know. We're at a loss. His liver is degenerating and we have no idea why. The only test left requires a biopsy, but hopefully, it will give us some definitive answers.

KATE. *(voice-over)* Then do it. Do it as soon as possible.

Scene Four

(KENDALL is practicing a dance in costume as "Will" that is the dance he and "Aunt Eller" will perform for their number "Kansas City".)

KENDALL. Gracie! Come on! We have to get this dance number down in costume. We were all over the place yesterday. Not good. We have to steal the show! We've never done it in costume and it's going to feel different. Trust me. *(dances some)* That's her downfall as a director. You need ring time. Everybody says so on *The Actor's Studio*. She never runs the whole play! *(dances more)* And you know how that Molly Miller isn't going to know all of her lines. She is so full of herself, with, well, I'm just going to say it, marginal talent at best. Gracie!

GRACIE. *(yelling offstage)* I look like a douche bag! Everybody's going to make fun of me.

KENDALL. People make fun of me all the time and I just ignore them. Remember, you are NOT Grace Westmoreland! You are "Aunt Eller".

GRACIE. *(yelling offstage)* Thanks for reminding me!

KENDALL. And I hate that Mrs. Lane doesn't make everybody be line perfect. *(imitating Mrs. Lane)* "Just get through it. Just get through it." I hate working with amateurs. I'm telling you, it feels very different in costume.

*(He twirls round and round, holding his chaps as **GRACIE** appears at the top of the stairs in a prairie outfit, bonnet, old lady glasses, gray wig. **KENDALL** looks up, suppresses laughter, knows better.)*

GRACIE. You laugh and I'll kill you!

KENDALL. I'm not laughing. You look…um, great!

GRACIE. Shut up, liar!

KENDALL. Come on! Let's just see if we can do it.

GRACIE. Okay.

(She clomps down the stairs.)

GRACIE. I swear to God, if Molly Miller messes up one of my scenes with her, I will...whatever...I'll be a professional like Meryl and cover for the little untalented bitch.

KENDALL. I can't wait 'til we get to NYU together and then become Broadway stars, then segue into film and TV, you know, if it's quality TV.

KENDALL/GRACIE. *(in unison)* Like *Glee*.

GRACIE. It has to be quality. I'd rather just skip TV altogether and win an Academy Award.

KENDALL. Well, that would be ideal. Like Barbra. She's never done TV. Except those specials. We start on Broadway, move to film, both win Oscars. This will be such a great story on *The Actor's Studio*. Oh! Maybe we can go on together! Oh, let's play *Actor's Studio*.

GRACIE. My turn to be the guest!

*(**KENDALL** rushes to the sofa, **GRACIE** pulls off the wig, puts it on the counter, rushes to make an entrance from the kitchen, they go into a familiar routine. **KENDALL** does his imitation of James Lipton, **GRACIE** her imitation of a star.)*

KENDALL. And now, *The Actor's Studio* is proud to present Grace Westmoreland.

GRACIE. Thank you, thank you, you are too kind. Everyone keep your seats, please.

(She sits.)

KENDALL. What is your favorite word?

GRACIE. "Yes".

KENDALL. What is your least favorite word?

GRACIE. "No".

KENDALL. What turns you on? What excites you? What inspires you?

GRACIE. Acting.

KENDALL. What turns you off?

GRACIE. Football.

KENDALL. What sound or noise do you love?

GRACIE. Children laughing.

KENDALL. What sound or noise do you hate?

GRACIE. Children crying.

KENDALL. What is your favorite curse word?

GRACIE. *(yelling)* FUCK!

KENDALL. *(overlap)* BEEP!

(They laugh.)

What profession other than your own would you like to attempt?

GRACIE. A diplomat. I would like to help heal this world, James.

KENDALL. *(hand over heart.)* So touching, so...*grace*ful.

GRACIE. Oh, James, you are so clever.

KENDALL. What profession would you not like to do?

GRACIE. Maggot farmer.

KENDALL. *(as* **KENDALL***)* Ewwww. That is so gross. *(back to James Lipton)* If Heaven exists, what would you like to hear God say when you arrive at the Pearly Gates?

GRACIE. "Grace Westmoreland, meet your biggest fan – Meryl Streep." *(suddenly hugs him)* Oh, Kendall Parker, I love you. You're the only one who gets me. I'm so glad you're my best friend.

KENDALL. *(a little taken aback)* Wow! Gracie. You're showing appreciation. That is so weird. It's like...I just have... you know, this thing, with you and your whole family. And Dayne...is like...my big brother, he always stood up for me when that mean pack of inbred idiots would make fun of me in gym class. Your family is the best.

GRACIE. Except lately. It's just us –

KENDALL. Well, with Dayne in the hospital, we can't be upset over your folks being gone to Jackson all the time.

GRACIE. No, we can't. I can't. It's not allowed. I have to act right. Behave. Not be selfish. And it is SO hard!

I'm basically raising myself lately...until he gets better
– or –

KENDALL. Don't say it!

GRACIE. It could happen. Mom and Dad sat me down and told me. It could really happen.

(silence)

KENDALL. I stopped praying when I was twelve years old. And nothing was different, nothing changed. I started thinking, when I was really little, how it didn't make sense. But I was so scared to question anything. Hell. *(bangs bass notes of piano)* The lake of fire. You know. I mean, puh-leeze, it's gotta be a really big place. I've never told anybody this, Gracie, but I think Mary was a slut!

GRACIE. Kendall!

KENDALL. Think about it. She was just covering up her pregnancy and they bought it! And what about Jesus is coming back soon? What exactly is the definition of "soon"? Okay, I mean, they say Jesus died and arose like over two thousand years ago – and he's coming back *(air quotes)* "soon"? I asked my mother what her definition of "soon" was once and she slapped me. When I was a kid, I believed all that, all that...stuff... and it scared me to death. I didn't want him to come back! I was just fine with the way things were.

GRACIE. I never think about any of that shit. We don't really get into all that at our church – plus, we never go. Especially not lately.

KENDALL. You are so lucky. *(long pause)* I started praying again. Every night.

GRACIE. Really? Why –

KENDALL. *(pause)* Because I don't want Dayne to die. So I started praying. Just in case. To God. To Jesus. And I pray, "If you are really real, prove it by making Dayne well. Because otherwise you are not real." A real God would save him, Gracie. He's too...perfect.

GRACIE. *(pause)* Yeah, the perfect child. Dayne. Robert Dayne Westmoreland, Jr. *(imitating a man)* "The apple doesn't fall too far from the tree." You know how many times I've heard that? Then there's me. *(pause)* One time I heard Mom talking on the phone to one of her friends and she said, "For everything I did good in my life, I got Dayne and for everything I did bad, I got Gracie." Then she laughed really hard. And I wondered…I wonder how many times she's said that – and laughed. It hurts my feelings. *(pause)* I think you are in love with my brother.

KENDALL. What?! No. I mean, I love him, *like* a brother, you know?

GRACIE. Kendall, you do know that you're gay.

KENDALL. *(pause)* No, I don't know. I mean, I'm not for sure.

GRACIE. Well, I sure hope you are. It's so scandalous and artistic. My favorite uncle is gay. Dad's brother Uncle Greg. I love him. You'll meet him when we move to New York. You should see his place. It is *so* clean. And when we get to New York, we can be roommates and live in the Village and nobody will make fun of you there. God, I hope you're gay. I think you are, Kendall.

KENDALL. We should practice the dance –

GRACIE. Thanks for praying for Dayne. Maybe I should start praying for my brother, too.

(They stand side by side and position themselves for the dance.)

KENDALL. And five six, here we go –

(They begin to dance a soft shoe essence to the beat of "Kansas City". They are not bad for high school choreography.)

One and da two da three da four da five six. Da one da two da three da four da five.

KENDALL/GRACIE. Da one da two da three and da five da six da seven. Da one da two and da three da four da five.

(TIMOTHEA enters, heads for the front door. She pauses a moment, looks up in prayer to heaven.)

TIMOTHEA. *(Calling, pounding on front door.)* Matthew Mark! Matthew Mark! Matthew Mark!

KENDALL. Oh shit! Shit! What am I going to do? She can't see me in my costume!

GRACIE. Go hide in Dayne's room. I'll get rid of her.

KENDALL. How?

GRACIE. I'm an actress! Go!

(KENDALL rushes up the stairs, enters Dayne's room. He sits on the bed in utter fear, puts his head in his hands. GRACIE answers the front door.)

GRACIE. Hello, Mrs. Parker.

(TIMOTHEA charges in, carrying her white bible.)

TIMOTHEA. Where is he?! Where is Matthew Mark, the deceiver?! *(TIMOTHEA begins searching the house.)* Matthew Mark! "Children obey your parents in the Lord: for this is right." Ephesians 6:1.

GRACIE. He's not here –

TIMOTHEA. You lie! "Thou shall not bear false witness." The ninth commandment, Grace Westmoreland.

(TIMOTHEA pulls out a crumpled up piece of paper from her pocket and waves it at GRACIE.)

Did he think I wouldn't find out? Did he think that God Almighty wouldn't direct me to the truth? *(shows flyer)* Thumb-tacked to the bulletin board at the Wash N Dry. *Oklahoma!?* Here's your name Grace Westmoreland! And here is his demonic name – which I refuse to speak!

GRACIE. He's not here and you have to leave. My parents –

TIMOTHEA. YOU LIE, LIAR!!!!

(KENDALL bolts up and rushes out of the room, down the stairs.)

KENDALL. *(calling)* Okay, I am! I am here! I'm here and I'm in the Fall musical!

TIMOTHEA. You will quit this.

KENDALL. No, I won't. I'm following my dream – !

TIMOTHEA. You will quit this!

KENDALL. No, I won't!

TIMOTHEA. Oh, yes you will! Yes, you will!!

(She rushes to KENDALL and starts slapping him. KENDALL guards his face.)

KENDALL. Mama, no, please –

GRACIE. Stop it! Stop it!

(The dialogue below is messy, overlapping [Although it is not, should feel like ad-libbing].)

TIMOTHEA. You have defied me –

KENDALL. I won't quit! I won't!

GRACIE. Stop! Don't hit him.

(GRACIE runs to the kitchen phone.)

TIMOTHEA. …You are on a path to destruction –

KENDALL. No, I'm not – !

(KENDALL falls, TIMOTHEA towers over him.)

TIMOTHEA. …and will burn for an eternity in hell – !

KENDALL. I won't quit! I won't!

GRACIE. *(phone in hand)* I'm calling my parents – !

TIMOTHEA. You will be separated from me and all of God's believers forever!

KENDALL. You can kill me, but I won't quit –

GRACIE. Stop! I'm calling the police!

TIMOTHEA. *(wheels on GRACIE)* You stay out of this, Grace Westmoreland!

(TIMOTHEA turns and charges KENDALL, begins slapping him repeatedly.)

GRACIE. *(screams)* Don't hit him! STOP!!!

TIMOTHEA. "He who spareth the rod hateth his son: but he that loveth him correcteth him betimes." Proverbs 13:24.

(slap, slap, slap)

(GRACIE *suddenly rushes over to* **TIMOTHEA** *and pulls her off of* **KENDALL. TIMOTHEA** *falls to the ground.)*

GRACIE. Leave him alone!

TIMOTHEA. *(to* **GRACIE***)* You have no right –

GRACIE. This is my house! Yes, I do! I do have a right!

TIMOTHEA. LIARS. DECEIVERS!

(TIMOTHEA *tries to get up, but before she does* **KENDALL** *rushes and towers over her.)*

KENDALL. I'm not going to hell! I'm not going to hell! And I'm going to tell! The school. The police. Everybody!

*(***TIMOTHEA** *rises.)*

TIMOTHEA. *(lethal)* You are *not* telling anyone.

KENDALL. I will. I'll tell them that you beat me! That you lock me in the closet to pray and tell me to search for Jesus. Well, guess what, Mama! I NEVER FOUND HIM!

TIMOTHEA. "He who spareth the rod hateth his son: but he that loveth him correcteth him betimes." Proverbs 13:24.

KENDALL. Gracie saw. Someone finally saw. They've made laws against your stupid Bible, Mama!

TIMOTHEA. BLASPHEMY! BLASPHEMY!

KENDALL. I'm going to tell! I mean it!

TIMOTHEA. *(low and seething)* You will not! You will do as I say. I am your mother. The vessel who brought you into this world. You will quit that play. That Devil's den of iniquity, and you will come home and pray and repent –

KENDALL. *(exploding)* No, I won't! I won't quit!

TIMOTHEA. And you will never return to this house of sinners –

KENDALL. *(calmer)* I will tell *everything*.

(TIMOTHEA *takes her white Bible, finds a scripture and reads.)*

TIMOTHEA. From the book of Deuteronomy: "If a man has a stubborn and rebellious son who does not obey his father and mother and will not listen to them when they discipline him, his father and mother shall take hold of him and bring him to the elders at the gate of his town. They shall say to the elders, This son of ours is stubborn and rebellious. He will not obey us. He is a profligate and a drunkard. Then all the men of his town shall stone him to death." The word of God.

GRACIE. You're crazy. You are so crazy.

TIMOTHEA. *(ignores* **GRACIE***, still with* **KENDALL***)* If you do not obey your mother and the Lord, if you do not repent and turn from this family of Episcopalian sinners and get on the path of righteousness, there will only be eternal damnation for you. If you do not turn and walk away, Matthew Mark, then you are no longer my son. You are no longer my child. And you are no longer a part of the family of God!

KENDALL. I'm not quitting the play. And if you make me, I'll tell everything. Everything.

TIMOTHEA. *(crying)* I must disown you now, Matthew Mark. You are a lost child. I must let you go. You are dead to me.

(She exits out the front door, **KENDALL** *right behind her.* **GRACIE** *rushes to the window and watches.)*

(porch)

KENDALL. Fine. Just leave. Leave! JUST LEAVE ME ALONE!

TIMOTHEA. *(turns back, low and lethal)* Your soul is in grave danger.

*(***TIMOTHEA** *exits,* **KENDALL** *watches her, then slowly returns to the house.)*

(Family room/kitchen. **KENDALL** *enters, then bursts into tears and sinks to the couch.* **GRACIE** *rushes to him, holds him.)*

KENDALL. There is no God, Gracie. If there was I wouldn't have a crazy Mother. *(softly)* And Dayne wouldn't be sick.

(blackout)

(during blackout)

SPECIALIST. *(voice-over)* Your son has a rare liver disease called primary sclerosing cholangitis – PSC. His liver is rapidly degenerating. Dying.

KATE. *(voice-over)* How did this happen? I don't –

SPECIALIST. *(voice-over)* The disease is so rare, we really don't know. He's most likely had it his entire life and was misdiagnosed as I.B.S.

BOBBY. *(voice-over)* What can you do? What can we do?

SPECIALIST. *(voice-over)* Unfortunately because of its rarity, there is no treatment and the only option for his survival…I'm sorry…is a transplant –

KATE. *(voice-over)* Bobby, tell me this isn't happening.

Scene Five

(Family room/kitchen. Lights come up on **BOBBY**, *who is sitting at the kitchen table on his laptop. He takes off his glasses, rubs his eyes, gets up and pours himself another cup of coffee, puts his glasses back on, takes a long swig, then continues to study his computer screen.* **KATE** *walks out of the bedroom in her robe.)*

KATE. Honey, it's almost three a.m.

BOBBY. I know. I'm almost done.

KATE. I'm going to sit on the porch. Look at the moon.

BOBBY. Tell my moon hello for me. And don't think I don't know what you're going to do out there.

*(***KATE*** doesn't respond, walks onto porch.* **KATE** *looks behind a plant, finds her hidden cigarettes and lighter, lights one, puts the package and matches back. She sits on the bench and stares at the moon.*

(Family room/kitchen. **BOBBY** *closes his computer, takes off his glasses, puts his cup on the counter, walks through the family room.)*

(Porch. **KATE** *drags on the cigarette as* **BOBBY** *walks out on the porch.* **KATE** *looks up at him, tears in her eyes.)*

BOBBY. Don't cry, Katie. And put that cigarette out. I don't like you smoking again. Plus, it makes you stink.

(He sits by her, puts his arm around her.)

You know what I think? I think there should be a quit smoking campaign where they don't talk about cancer or heart attacks or health, they just say, "You should quit smoking. Because you *stink!*"

*(***KATE*** smiles weakly as* **BOBBY** *gets up, paces, wired.)*

He's going to make it, Katie. I just read everything there is to read on the internet about it. There are dads who saved their children, brothers who saved their brother or sister, moms who saved their kid. Hell, there's a guy up in Toronto who had Hepatitis C for years, then his liver played out and his twenty-six-year-old son gave him half of his liver and they both are just fine now. They've made lots of progress with living donors and the medications, so our boy is going to have a normal life. And so will I. He's gonna play football again and our lives will get right back on track.

KATE. You've had too much coffee. You are so wired.

BOBBY. I know. I'll never get to sleep now. Not that I sleep lately. How is it I didn't know my own blood type at age forty-two?

KATE. You never had a reason to know. The only reason I know is because I gave mother blood when she needed that transfusion. Lots of people don't know.

BOBBY. *(still wired)* So, listen. You're A, Dayne's B. That means I'm either B or AB. And odds are I'm B. Ten percent of the population are B, four percent AB. Over twice the odds if my math skills are right. I'm getting smarter by the minute, Katie. Hell, I could teach Biology next year. I'm gonna match, Katie. I feel it. Hell, I don't want some ol' stray dead person's liver in my son. And if it were you – um, were subjunctive tense. See, gettin' smarter every day. *(smiles, proud of himself, then serious)* Gracie and Kendall need you and it's easier for me to take the time off. You have screwed up patients to help. How can they live without their savior?

KATE. You are *so* wired.

BOBBY. Besides, they don't let smokers donate.

*(**KATE** gets up to put out the cigarette.)*

KATE. I'm not a real smoker. I'm not a real smoker anymore.

BOBBY. I know, baby. You're stressed. We all are. But you should start jogging again. Take one of the pills the doc gave you. Something besides those cancer sticks. Makes me worry harder. Plus, you stink.

(He chuckles, squeezes her arm, reaches over and kisses her cheek. It's too much. **KATE** *suddenly gets ups, paces a moment, then backs against the wall and starts crying.* **BOBBY** *gets up, starts for her.)*

BOBBY. Aw, honey, stop.

KATE. No, Bobby, don't. Don't touch me. Don't be sweet to me. Don't be nice to me. I can't take it –

BOBBY. But –

KATE. *(upset)* Just stop talking, please! I need you to stop talking. I need to speak. I need to talk to you. Please. Just don't say anything until I'm done because this is important and I need to – !

BOBBY. Okay.

*(***KATE*** takes several deep breaths, braces herself, looks away, takes another deep breath, then turns to* **BOBBY.***)*

KATE. You're not a match, Bobby.

BOBBY. What?

KATE. You won't be a match tomorrow when they test your blood. You won't be a match. I know your blood type, Bobby. It's A. Just like mine. You're A. You're not a match.

BOBBY. I didn't mean to upset you –

KATE. Let me talk, Bobby. Just sit there, please and don't say anything until I finish.

BOBBY. Okay, please. *(sits)* I'm just so…confused.

KATE. I don't know how many times as a therapist, I've given the same advice that I gave to myself so many years ago. Don't tell. There's no reason to tell. It'll just hurt. It'll destroy. It'll just…just guard the secret, try to make peace with yourself…although it's next to impossible…and love harder. Love hard the one you could have hurt. The one you betrayed. That's what I tell my patients. That's what I told myself. And I never thought – *(pause)* It all started that first year we were married. When I was still teaching here in Vicksburg and you were in Denver playing for the Broncos. I was a newlywed who never saw her new husband. It was so…wrong. But you were gone and I was…young…and stupid…and careless. I knew I should stop, we should stop…but I couldn't. Billy was here and you were there… and I was…weak. I'm strong now…well, not now…I'm weak again…but I was weak back then. So weak. And I was lonely. *(pause)* Remember when I surprised you that one weekend. There was a blizzard in Denver. I almost didn't get there. They cancelled all the flights right after…but I made it. And you were so excited to see me. We made love all weekend…but it was all calculated. The visit. I knew…that I was already pregnant. It…it was…a cover-up. That way you could trace back and know when he was conceived…and never doubt…but, it was…deception. So you wouldn't know the awful thing that I did. That I couldn't take back. Billy never knew either. He died not knowing. That weekend…he thought Dayne happened that weekend. Only me. Only I knew. My secret. My dark, dark secret that I kept for almost nineteen years. So it wouldn't destroy…it wouldn't hurt the most important person in my life. *(whispers)* You. *(Silence. Long silence.)* You won't be a match, Bobby. You're not a match. *(tears flowing)* You can't save him, Bobby. Dayne is not your son.

(**BOBBY** *gets up and walks back into the house without looking back. Lights fade as* **KATE** *crumbles on the bench, destroyed.)*

(blackout)

END OF ACT ONE

ACT TWO

Scene One

(In darkness, the play ends.)

CAST. *(voice-over)* "O.K. L – A – H – O – M – A, Oklahoma! Yeeow!"

(Applause. Cheering.)

BOBBY. *(voice-over)* That's my girl, Gracie! Best Aunt Eller ever! Go Will! *(whistles)* Way to go, Kendall!

(Parents applaud and cheer.)

(Dayne's room. Lights come up. **DAYNE** *is asleep. He is noticeably more jaundiced [with make-up]. He tosses, turns, moans.)*

(Porch. Lights come up. It's night. **KATE** *sits on the bench, smoking. The front door is cracked open.)*

(Dayne's room. He wakes up, breathing hard.)

DAYNE. *(disoriented.)* Mom…Dad…Mom…? *(He reaches over with great effort, picks up a bell on the nightstand and rings it.)* Mom –

(Porch. **KATE** *hears the bell, puts out her cigarette, quickly hides the package and lighter, rushes into the house.)*

(Family room. **KATE** *enters, bounds up the stairs.)*

KATE. I'm coming. I'm coming, honey.

(Dayne's room. **KATE** *arrives, enters.)*

What's wrong? You okay?

DAYNE. I had that dream again. That bad dream.

*(He holds his pillow, breathing hard. **KATE** sits on the bed, takes his hand.)*

KATE. Oh, honey. It wasn't real. You know it wasn't real.

DAYNE. I know, I know. It just feels so real when I'm dreamin'. Oh Mom, I'm so tired. Of everything. *(tries to laugh)* This is not how I thought I'd spend my senior year.

KATE. I know, sweetie. And I'm sorry. But you're home now, and pretty soon it's all going to be okay because you're going to get –

DAYNE. I know. It just sucks, that's all. That's all. And it's so stupid that you have to almost die before you get to the top of that list. And it's weird that someone I don't know has to die so I don't have to.

KATE. We're putting the word out. You know your dad and I wanted to donate so bad…but he's the wrong blood type, I'm not the right size – and Gracie's too young –

DAYNE. I don't want part of Gracie's liver. I don't want meanness transplanted into me.

KATE. Now, now. Gracie's trying real hard to be nice and is doing so much better.

DAYNE. I'm not really scared to die, Mom.

KATE. You're not going to die, so don't even talk about it.

DAYNE. But in my dreams, it's scary. Not that I'm dead. I'm buried alive. Now that's scary. *(joking)* Don't let them bury me alive, Mama.

KATE. This is a non-issue. I'm going to be long gone before you. Parents are supposed to die before their children and that's the way it's going to be.

(She gives him a pill from the many bottles sitting on the nightstand and lifts a glass for him to swallow with a straw.)

(smiles) Mama. You haven't called me Mama since you were…well, I can't remember since when.

(She slides up next to him, puts her arm around her boy, strokes his hair.)

KATE. *(cont.)* You've always had nightmares. Ever since you were just a little bitty thing. To this day, I could kill your Granddaddy Fuller for telling you there was a boogyman.

DAYNE. *(joking)* You mean, there's not?

KATE. How do you do that?

DAYNE. What?

KATE. Have a sense of humor these days. I don't think I've laughed since that night I noticed you were yellow. *(pause, smiles)* Hey, your birthday's coming up in a couple of months. You're going to be an adult.

DAYNE. I sure don't feel much like an adult.

KATE. For as long as you can, don't!

DAYNE. You need to laugh, Mom. I'm going to tell you a joke. A dirty joke.

KATE. A dirty joke?

DAYNE. Yeah, I want to make you laugh.

KATE. And you think my son telling me a dirty joke will do the trick? I don't think so.

DAYNE. Don't be such a prude. And don't think of me as your son. Think of me as your friend...the adult who likes to tell you dirty jokes.

KATE. *(smiles)* I'll try.

DAYNE. There were these three nuns –

KATE. Oh no. Not a nun joke.

DAYNE. Shhh! Okay, see, there were these three nuns who were waiting for confession and they were really, really nervous. So the first nun goes in that booth thingie and says, "Forgive me Father for I have sinned." And the ol' padre says, "Tell me your sin, Sister." And the nun says, "Well...I saw a man's penis."

KATE. Dayne!

DAYNE. Shhh. You're ruining the flow. So the priest says, "You must say ten Hail Marys and wash your eyes out with holy water." So the second nun comes into the booth and says, "Forgive me Father, for I have sinned."

"Yes, Sister, tell me your sins." "Well, I...I touched a man's penis." –

(**KATE** *makes a sound.*)

...And the priest, you know, was trying not to be appalled 'cause he was just doing his job and stuff and he said, "Sister! You must go immediately and say one hundred Hail Marys and wash your hands with holy water." "Yes, Father, thank you." So as the second nun was leaving, the third nun, who had been eavesdropping – you know, like nuns do – yells out, "Hey, Sister, don't get soap in that holy water. I may have to gargle."

(**KATE** *bursts out laughing,* **DAYNE** *follows suit.*)

KATE. Oh, that's awful.

DAYNE. Awfully funny. I made you laugh.

KATE. Who told you that?!

DAYNE. Dad. When I was about fourteen years old.

(*Offstage. Car pulls up, three doors slam.*)

KATE. Oh, that Daddy of yours.

(*Offstage.* **BOBBY**, **GRACIE** *and* **KENDALL** *sing.*)

BOBBY, GRACIE, AND KENDALL. And when we say, Yeeow! Aye-yip-aye-yo-ee-ay!

KATE. Well, I believe they are home.

(*Porch.* **BOBBY**, **GRACIE** *and* **KENDALL** *enter, walk towards the front door.*)

BOBBY, GRACIE AND KENDALL. O.K. L – A – H – O – M – A, Oklahoma! Yeeow!

(*Dayne's room.*)

DAYNE. Help me up, Mom. I wanna go downstairs.

KATE. You sure?

DAYNE. Yeah, I want to hear about the play.

KATE. Okay.

(Family room. **BOBBY**, **GRACIE** *and* **KENDALL** *enter the family room.)*

BOBBY. *(overlap)* Well, that was a brilliant production. Two amazing performances and the stars are right here in my house. I can't believe how much I like a play with the same name as a state I don't much care for.

KENDALL. What's wrong with Oklahoma?

BOBBY. The people. *(whispers)* Trashy.

KENDALL. Trashier than people in Mississippi?

BOBBY. Oh God, yes! But not as bad as folks from Alabama. And Louisiana. Whoo! Trash off the charts.

(They laugh. **BOBBY** *looks up and sees* **KATE** *helping* **DAYNE** *down the stairs.)*

DAYNE. Hey Dad, hey guys, hold on Mom, I'm dizzy.

BOBBY. Well, looky here. You coming down to visit, son?

DAYNE. I want to hear about the play.

GRACIE. I can't believe that you're remotely interested in anything in my life.

DAYNE. She ain't trying that hard to be nice.

KATE. "Isn't." She "isn't" trying that hard to be nice.

DAYNE. Oh Mom, please. People with liver diseases don't have to have good grammar.

BOBBY. That's right. I believe there's actually a scripture in the Bible about it. Somewhere in Titus. *(***BOBBY** *starts up the stairs.)* Here, let me help him.

KATE. It's okay, I got him.

BOBBY. *(terse)* Let me help my boy down. *(realizing)* I mean, you must be tired. I have all this energy after seeing a musical that could have been on Broadway.

*(***BOBBY** *leads* **DAYNE** *to the couch,* **KATE** *fluffs the pillows.)*

GRACIE. Oh, please, you can stop. Molly Miller forgot half her lines and made up the other half.

KENDALL. Amateur. Marginal talent.

GRACIE. I would have kicked ass as "Laurie". Mrs. Lane is so going to regret this when I'm starring on Broadway.

KATE. Oh, I can't wait to see it tomorrow.

KENDALL. You need anything, Dayne. A glass of water? A sandwich? I can make macaroni and cheese.

DAYNE. No, I'm good, thanks. But I'll take a rain check on the mac and cheese. That's my favorite.

KENDALL. Mine too!

KATE. He had some soup. Not much. But he did eat.

BOBBY. That's good, that's good.

(**KATE** *puts her hand on* **BOBBY**'s *shoulder. He flinches.*)

KATE. So, the play was good?

(**BOBBY** *gets up, moves away from* **KATE**.)

BOBBY. No, it wasn't good, it was great. I think I'll have a sandwich.

KATE. I can do that.

BOBBY. No! I'll do it myself. I've got all this energy. I saw this musical that coulda been on Broadway.

GRACIE. Okay, Dad, we got it.

DAYNE. Hey, Gracie, Kendall. I had a great idea for a musical that you can write.

(**KENDALL** *joins* **DAYNE** *on the couch.*)

KENDALL. Oh, I've always planned to write a musical. I'd love to collaborate. We can work on it for hours and hours and it'll help you pass the time while you wait and I'd love to hang out and you know, write it with you.

GRACIE. Oh brother. He said Gracie and Kendall, not just you, Kendall!

KENDALL. You're welcome to collaborate with us, right Dayne? She writes great poetry. *(whispers)* Although, it is a little dark and twisted.

GRACIE. Shut up, Kendall.

KENDALL. So what's your idea?

DAYNE. It's about me. When I get a new liver.

GRACIE. Oh great. I'm sure it'll be a big hit. A musical about getting a liver.

DAYNE. Yeah! And I have the perfect title. You ready?

KENDALL. *(with enthusiam)* Yes! I'm ready.

GRACIE. Kendall, he's not serious, so you're not going to spend hours and hours with him writing a musical. About a liver.

DAYNE. I'm dead serious. 'Cause see, in the musical, "Dayne" the handsome studly lead of the musical – played by Kendall here – gets a new liver and everybody lives happily ever after. You wanna hear the title?

KENDALL. I do!

BOBBY. What's the title, son?

DAYNE. *(Supressing a laugh)* "De*livered!*"

(A pause. Then one by one everybody starts laughing except **GRACIE.***)*

BOBBY. That's a good one, son.

GRACIE. I don't get it.

KENDALL. De – livered!? It's brilliant!

*(***KATE*** looks at* **BOBBY** *as they all laugh. Then* **BOBBY** *and* **KATE** *lock eyes and* **BOBBY** *stops laughing. Then* **KATE.** **BOBBY** *dismisses the moment.)*

(Porch. **TIMOTHEA** *walks up to the porch and rings the doorbell.)*

KATE. Who is that?

*(***GRACIE*** looks out the window.)*

GRACIE. It's Kendall's crazy mother.

KATE. Great –

KENDALL. Oh, no.

KATE. Don't worry.

*(***KATE*** opens the door,* **BOBBY** *following her out. He closes the door behind them as they usher* **TIMOTHEA** *away from the door. Inside* **KENDALL** *and* **GRACIE** *look out the window.)*

KATE. What do you want, Timothea?!

KENDALL. Go away. Go away.

DAYNE. Come here, Kendall. Mom and Dad will handle your mother.

*(**KENDALL** walks over to **DAYNE**, sits by him.)*

BOBBY. Because if you are here for Kendall, you are going to have to get through me.

*(**DAYNE** puts his arm around **KENDALL**.)*

TIMOTHEA. "Be ye not unequally yoked together with unbelievers: for what fellowship hath righteousness with unrighteousness." Second Corinithians 6:14.

DAYNE. Don't worry, buddy.

TIMOTHEA. *(emotional)* It's too late to save Matthew Mark. Our God almighty has told me that I have obeyed his word and let him go.

KATE. Unbelievable –

TIMOTHEA. But it's not too late to save your own son. The Lord spoke to me and told me to lay hands on young Dayne and heal him.

KATE. He what?!

TIMOTHEA. I am a healer, Kate Westmoreland. The Lord uses me as an instrument to heal the sick and the afflicted. These are healing hands. God instructs me as to who to heal. *(pause)* And he has chosen your son, Dayne Westmoreland.

KATE. You are delusional.

*(Family room/kitchen. **DAYNE** lies his head down on the arm of the couch. **KENDALL** gets a pillow and puts it under **DAYNE**'s head during:)*

(porch)

TIMOTHEA. May I please come in and obey God Almighty and heal your ailing son. Like Jesus healed the lepers and raised Lazarus from the dead?

BOBBY. I think you should leave now.

KATE. No, you cannot come in! You are not about to expose all your bullshit to my son, who is fighting for his life.

GRACIE. I can't hear what they're saying, but Mom's getting pissed!

(**KENDALL** *rushes over, looks out the window again with* **GRACIE**.)

TIMOTHEA. *(begins to preach, raises her hand to heavens)* There is sin in this house!

KATE. Stop it!

BOBBY. Okay, you have to leave –

TIMOTHEA. God took the son of David unto death, the son he conceived with Bathsheba, the wife of Uriah, who David had killed in battle to steal another man's wife. As punishment God took David's son. The Lord is speaking to me and telling me of your sins. *(listens, then realizes and points directly to* **KATE***)* Your sin is the reason your boy is sick!

KATE. Just shut up!

(She bounds for **TIMOTHEA**, **BOBBY** *holds* **KATE** *back.)*

BOBBY. You have to leave now.

TIMOTHEA. I will. I will leave, but when you listen to God Almighty speaking through me and allow him to love and heal your son by me laying on hands, anointing him with the spirit, that's when you will raise your son from impending death –

KATE. How dare you! You're the worst mother who ever lived, beating that beautiful boy of yours! I'm a good mother! I'm a good mother. Bobby, get her out of here. *(angry emotion)* I'm a good mother!

(**BOBBY** *starts escorting* **TIMOTHEA** *away.*)

BOBBY. Get! And don't you ever come back. I mean it.

TIMOTHEA. Do not touch me, Bobby Westmoreland. I will leave on my own accord. But God will lead you to the light and you will know this is the only way to save your son. I beg of you, do not take the risk. What do you have to lose?

KATE. Just leave, you crazy woman!

(TIMOTHEA raises her hands to the heavens.)

TIMOTHEA. His blood is on your hands, Kate Westmoreland!

KATE. Get out! Get out!!

(KATE screams and starts for TIMOTHEA. BOBBY grabs KATE, blocking her.)

TIMOTHEA. *(as she exits)* His blood is on your hands.

(KATE collapses into BOBBY's arms. An uncomfortable moment for BOBBY. He pulls her off of him.)

BOBBY. Come on.

(He leads KATE back to sit on the porch bench.)

It's bullshit. She's crazy.

KATE. Bobby, it's not true, is it? Do you think the Lord told her? Is Dayne sick because…It's not true, is it?

(BOBBY stares at KATE for a long moment.)

BOBBY. No, it's not true. Just sit here and get a hold of yourself.

(BOBBY enters the house. KENDALL rushes over.)

KENDALL. Thank you for not letting her take me.

BOBBY. She's never going to take you. *(pause, pulls KENDALL in for a hug)* Kendall, I want you to call me Dad. You are part of this family now. *(He looks over at DAYNE asleep on the table.)* You don't have to be blood to be family. I want you to call me Dad.

KENDALL. *(nods)* Okay…Dad.

(GRACIE goes and hugs BOBBY.)

(KATE sits on the porch, recovering. She takes a deep breath, wipes her eyes. As she walks towards the front door, lights fade.)

(blackout)

(in blackout)

SPECIALIST. *(voice-over)* Your son is in very grave condition. He's being moved to the top of the waiting list, but he has the second rarest blood type –

KATE. *(voice-over)* We know all that! Just do something. You have to find –

SPECIALIST. *(voice-over)* Mrs. Westmoreland, last year alone there were over 16,000 people on the transplant list and only around 6,000 transplants. We're doing the best that we can, but –

KATE. *(voice-over)* I don't need your statistics, I need you to save my son. Why are you telling me this?

BOBBY. *(voice-over)* You just have to find a donor! We have to find a donor! He's not even eighteen years old. I'll do anything. Pay anything.

SPECIALIST. *(voice-over)* I've recommended that he be moved to the top of the list. That's all I can do, right now. And hope. And pray.

Scene Two

*(Porch. **KATE** sits in her robe, smoking. She puts out a cigarette, stares at the sky.)*

*(Dayne's room. **BOBBY** passes Dayne's room in the hall, in warm-ups and an Ole Miss T-shirt. He pauses, looks at his boy, then enters, readjusts his covers, strokes his boy's hair. He continues down the stairs, sees **KATE** through the window sitting on the porch, smoking. He pauses, stares at **KATE** for a moment, then walks through the family room and exits onto the porch.)*

*(Porch. **BOBBY** walks out, sits on the railing.)*

BOBBY. Can't sleep?

*(**KATE** shakes her head.)*

Yeah, me too.

KATE. I need you to be mad at me, Bobby. I need you to yell and scream and tell me what a horrible person I am. I just need to talk about it. Please. Something. Say something. Anything.

BOBBY. I can't do it.

KATE. You have to, Bobby. Otherwise, it'll just fester. Inside you. And you'll breed resentment and hatred –

BOBBY. Please don't psychoanalyze me, Kate. I don't give a shit if you are a therapist, if you do have a master's degree and I don't care how smart you are. I'm not your patient. And you have no idea what's going on inside me. What I'm really going through.

KATE. This is good –

BOBBY. *(snapping)* Stop it! *(deep breath)* I won't go there. I won't. I can't, Kate. I can't.

KATE. Why? Bottling it up inside isn't healthy –

BOBBY. *(pause)* Because if I go there, I'll say things…I'll have to…I won't be able to…I need to put every ounce of my energy into saving Dayne. My son. Yeah, he's mine, Kate –

KATE. Of course he is –

BOBBY. You can't take that away. That hasn't changed. And he always will be. To the day I die. That boy is mine. *(controlled anger)* I may not have been the fuck that brought him into this world, but he is my son. He is my boy. He is attached to my heart and my soul. And I don't know how to be…I don't know how to live… without that. Without him. Without being his father. And Gracie's. And now poor little Kendall. And I will never give that up, Kate –

KATE. Please call me Katie. You haven't called me Katie since –

BOBBY. I can't. I'm sorry. Katie is…was…the love of my life. My wife. My partner. The mother of my children who told me the truth. From the day we met. No secrets. No lies. The perfect couple. The perfect family. I believed that. But…it wasn't…it was all a sham. Pure and utter bullshit.

KATE. No –

BOBBY. Yes! It was! Do you know how I've relived every moment, every memory since you told me. Every fishing trip with Billy. Every conversation. With him. With you. The birth of our son. Then our daughter. Wondering – did anybody else know? Did God really speak to Timothea or does she know? Does the town know? Did you tell anyone?

KATE. No, I didn't –

BOBBY. How am I supposed to believe that? How am I supposed to believe anything, Kate? Huh? You were able to lie to me for years! Almost nineteen goddamn years. And is there someone in this town who saw? Who knew? Did Billy tell? Brag about banging his best friend's wife? Have I been a laughing stock for nineteen years? Where did he park his car? How long did he stay? All night? Was he holding my wife all night? Waking up in my bed, drinking my booze, because we know how Billy loved his booze – the reason he died.

Drinking and driving. Did it ever happen again? Was he better than me in bed? Was his dick bigger?! And how the hell do I reconcile – even if I could reconcile his being the fuck, the biological fuck. Not father. Not dad. Not daddy. And I can't even tell the son-of-a-bitch off! I can't even beat the shit out of him. That sorry biological fuck can't even save our son –

KATE. Stop – !

BOBBY. Oh, I thought you wanted this. I thought this would help. To get it out. Show my anger. Tell you how my entire being is churning…churning like a goddamn washing machine. When I should be putting every ounce of energy into saving my son. And you think I didn't have opportunity? I was a NFL player before I wrecked my knee. With looks and a body. I had women throwing themselves at me, but…I would have never…I could never…because I couldn't bear to hurt you…and I didn't want anybody else. *(pause)* So, you got it, okay? You did it. You made me spew. Purge. Spit it all out, letting you know how pissed off…how fucking angry I am at you. And at Billy. Billy for dying. And you for living. To tell me. Yeah harsh, huh? He probably could have saved my son. But he was a goddamn loser and lost his own life because he was careless. Precious life. A drunk. My best friend who 'til the day he died couldn't get his shit together. Died owing me ten grand. Took money from the man whose wife he fucked! What kind of person was he? And you, Kate? What kind of human being could do what you did?

KATE. I was young –

BOBBY. And stupid and weak. Yeah, I heard it. *(pause)* And then I go to that place of Dayne wouldn't exist if you hadn't done it. If Billy hadn't. And that's what I focus on, Kate. Because I can't imagine life without that boy. *(chokes up)* And yet that is such a possibility now and I don't know how to go on – yet I have to. For Gracie. For Kendall. For Dayne. To save him… *(realization)* or to honor him if we can't. But I don't feel I have to go on for you, Kate. Not anymore. And…I don't want to touch you or hold you – even though I should because you're hurting too – and now I'm hurting you more. My head says that I can't negate those years, those happy years where I loved you so hard I sometimes hurt. Where I'd wake up and watch you sleep and feel so completely content…and safe…but not knowing the truth. And I wish Katie…Kate…that Dayne had never gotten sick. Because I would rather have died never knowing this awful, painful truth…and…and I would never have stopped loving you –

(long pause)

KATE. So do you not love me anymore?

BOBBY. I don't know how not to. And I don't know how to. *(pause)* I have to be done with this…this conversation… these endless thoughts. They are toxic. And I need to put every ounce of energy into hope…and prayer…to save my son. My son.

*(**BOBBY** walks back into the house, leaving **KATE** sitting on the bench, destroyed.)*

(blackout)

(in blackout)

(These prayers should all overlap.)

KENDALL. *(voice-over)* Dear Father, please make Dayne well again. He's so perfect and good and I have faith, I really do that you can heal him –

GRACIE. *(voice-over)* …and of course I really would like you to help me become a really famous actress, but most of all…the most important thing of all is my brother. Make him okay and I promise I'll be nicer –

KATE. *(voice-over)* I'm trying so hard not to be angry, God, but it is so hard. If this is my fault, then make it about me, punish me, not my son. I'm just asking that you be a fair God and –

BOBBY. *(voice-over)* ...and I'll get back in church, be a better person, if you'll just heal my son...I'll do anything. Anything... Oh God –

TIMOTHEA. *(in darkness)* Oh God, I call on you, on your healing powers to heal this boy, this child of yours. To wash his young soul in the blood of the Lamb.

Scene Three

(Dayne's room. Lights come up. **TIMOTHEA** *is standing over* **DAYNE**, *who sits on the edge of his bed. One hand is on his head, the other is stretched towards heaven, white Bible in it.* **BOBBY** *stands on the other side of* **DAYNE**, *both hands on his son. There is a noticeable change in* **DAYNE**. *When he speaks, it's with great effort. He is much weaker.)*

TIMOTHEA. Forgive the transgressions of the parents. Do not punish this child any longer for their sins. Save this boy and let him live to tell the story of this healing, to witness to others, to save the lives, to save other lost souls.

*(***DAYNE*** looks up at his dad.)*

DAYNE. *(almost pleading)* Dad –

BOBBY. Shh. Let's just try, son –

(Porch. Lights come up as a car drives up. Three car doors slam.)

(Dayne's room. **TIMOTHEA** *begins to work herself into a frenzy.)*

TIMOTHEA. Heal him, Lord! Heal him, Lord!! Heal your son, Dayne Westmoreland. *(waving the Bible)* "Where two or three are gathered together in my name there am I in the middle of them." Matthew 18:20.

(Porch. **GRACIE**, **KENDALL** *and* **KATE** *approach the house.* **KATE** *juggles two bags of groceries.)*

KATE. Kendall, sweetie, take this bag, please.

KENDALL. Yes, ma'am.

(Dayne's room.)

TIMOTHEA. Do you believe, Bobby Westmoreland. Do you believe?

BOBBY. Yes, I believe.

(Porch. **KENDALL** *takes a bag from* **KATE**.*)*

KENDALL. Can I help cook?

KATE. Sure, you can make the salad and mac and cheese.

(Dayne's room.)

TIMOTHEA. Do you believe, Dayne Westmoreland?

DAYNE. *(weakly)* Yes, I believe.

TIMOTHEA. *(overlap)* "And the Lord said, if ye have faith the size of a mustard seed ye could say to the sycamine tree…"

(Porch. **KATE,** **GRACIE** *and* **KENDALL** *enter.)*

(Family room/kitchen. **KATE** *hears* **TIMOTHEA.***)*

KATE. No.

KENDALL. Mother?

GRACIE. Oh, shit!

(Family room/kitchen. **KATE** *hands her bag of groceries to* **GRACIE** *and bounds up the stairs as* **TIMOTHEA** *begins speaking in tongues.)*

(Dayne's room. **KATE** *bursts through the door.)*

KATE. What the hell is going on?! Bobby – ?

BOBBY. I had to try. We have to try everything –

TIMOTHEA. Join us, Kate Westmoreland and heal your son!

KATE. No – !

BOBBY. I asked her here.

DAYNE. *(tears in his eyes)* Mom, don't be mad at Dad. He was just –

KATE. I don't care! This is bullshit! Stupidity! We are not ignorant people! He's crying, Bobby. Get out! Get out of my home!!

*(***TIMOTHEA** *exits, lifting her hands to the heavens.* **KATE** *wheels on* **BOBBY.***)*

BOBBY. Kate –

KATE. Behind my back, Bobby? How?

BOBBY. I want to save him –

KATE. And you really think this voodoo, woowoo backwoods horsecrap will work? All she needed were snakes to handle!

BOBBY. I don't know. I just want to try anything –

KATE. Me too, Bobby, but this isn't –

DAYNE. *(big effort)* Mom! *(worn out)* Don't be mad. He…Dad was –

KATE. Shh, shh. Let's just get you back in bed.

(Family room/kitchen. **TIMOTHEA** *is watching* **KENDALL***'s back from the stairs. She comes down the stairs, crosses to the door and turns back.)*

TIMOTHEA. I miss you, son.

GRACIE. Well, Kendall doesn't miss you.

KENDALL. If I'm dead, then why are you talking to a corpse?

TIMOTHEA. Come home. Come home to your mother. Come home to Jesus!!

(Dayne's room. **KATE** *hears* **TIMOTHEA** *and flies out of the room.)*

(Family room/kitchen. **KATE** *charges at* **TIMOTHEA** *across the family room.)*

KATE. Get out! Get out of my house!!!

DAYNE. Dad!

*(***BOBBY*** comes after* **KATE** *as* **TIMOTHEA** *exits.* **KATE** *slams the door.)*

BOBBY. Stop it! You're stressing him out. The doctor said –

KATE. And what you did, didn't? He was crying, Bobby. That pressure. I know the drill. Have faith or it won't work. I know you were brought up with that bullshit, but I wasn't.

BOBBY. Let's just talk on the front porch.

KATE. Fine, let's. I'm going to make sure he's okay first.

*(***BOBBY*** starts out the door.)*

GRACIE. Dad –

BOBBY. Not now! Not now, angel face. I need to step out and get some air. Kendall, I didn't mean for you to see your mother. I though we'd be done –

KENDALL. It's okay, you were just...hoping.

BOBBY. Yeah –

KENDALL. Come on, Gracie. Help me with my mac and cheese.

(BOBBY exits as GRACIE and KENDALL work in the kitchen.)

Let's remember all this. We can draw on it in our acting.

(Dayne's room. KATE straightens Dayne's covers.)

DAYNE. Everybody...has to believe. It doesn't work if...I tried. *(closes eyes, mutters)* Don't...be hard...on Dad –

(He drifts off. KATE kisses him.)

KATE. *(quietly)* My baby. My baby boy.

(She kisses him again, then exits. As she walks down the stairs –)

(Family room/kitchen.)

(KATE heads towards the porch, glances at the kitchen.)

Gracie, set the table.

GRACIE. Did the word "please" just evaporate from your vocabulary?

KATE. Gracie. Set the table, please.

GRACIE. *(softens)* Is Dayne – ?

KATE. He's not doing well, Gracie.

GRACIE. Okay. Dad's really upset.

KATE. I know.

(As KATE exits onto the porch, GRACIE runs to the window and stares out, hiding from her parents. KENDALL continues to work in the kitchen.)

(Porch. BOBBY is pacing. KATE goes right for the hidden cigarettes.)

BOBBY. You're just going to light up? The kids are home –
KATE. Yeah, I am.
BOBBY. What a great example.
KATE. Well, at least I'm showing them that they have one parent who is still sane.

(**KATE** *takes out a cigarette, lights it, sits on the bench.*)

Did he eat?
BOBBY. No. And yes, I've gone crazy, Kate. Completely insane. I've lost my mind trying to save him.
KATE. Did you at least try and feed him or was this healing bullshit more important than basic needs that will keep him – ?
BOBBY. Just stop – !
KATE. How could you? Behind my back? I am so mad at you.
BOBBY. *(snaps)* Behind *your* back? You're mad at me? You have a lot of gall. After what you did behind my back, you're mad. Unbelievable –
KATE. That has nothing to do with this. Don't you bring that up. Stick to the subject.
BOBBY. Timothea says it does.
KATE. If those kooks could heal, Bobby, then why don't you ever see amputees growing limbs, huh? And you had no right to bring up –
BOBBY. I had no right? I had no right? Well, you brought him into our bed, so that negates any rights that you –
KATE. What?! You *have* gone crazy!

(*Family room/kitchen.* **GRACIE** *continues to try and listen.* **KENDALL** *pours noodles from a Kraft box into boiling water.*)

KENDALL. What are they saying?
BOBBY. *(overlap)* I admitted that!
GRACIE. *(overlap)* I can't hear, but they are fighting big time.

(**KENDALL** *comes over, joins* **GRACIE**, *trying to eavesdrop as the argument heats up.*)

KATE. So, you get to dictate that I've lost my rights as his mother – ?

BOBBY. Yeah, I get to "dictate" whatever I goddamn please now –

KATE. I see. And I don't have any say anymore –

BOBBY. No! As a matter of fact, you don't, Kate! You forfeited your rights the day you...I was just trying to save my son! I'll try anything, Kate. If I have to sacrifice a lamb, burn an ox on an altar, cut off my right arm, my left nut, whatever it takes. I can't lose him, Kate. I can't. So, be mad. You be mad! I've gone mad! It's a mad, mad world!

(**KATE** *softens, puts out the cigarette, gets up, goes to him.*)

KATE. I know this is hard, honey. You're just working through –

BOBBY. Don't be my therapist! Goddamn you!

KATE. *(pause)* Okay, I'm sorry.

(*She touches his arm. He pulls it away.*)

BOBBY. And don't touch me! Don't call me "honey". Just don't! Don't! God, I hate being around you!

KATE. Okay, fine! *(pause)* You may think you can dictate my rights, that I have forfeited for my horrible crime... and yes, it was horrible, Bobby, but what you did was damaging to our son! She can't heal him. *It's not possible!* And to put that pressure on that sick boy, to ask him to believe the unbelievable...and you know damn well that you don't believe that crap anymore either, Bobby –

BOBBY. Okay, okay, I fucked up! I fucked up, okay?! So just shut up. Shut up! Because if you don't, I will do something, I will say something...something awful, something mean and harmful that will hurt –

KATE. *(through tears)* There is nothing! NOTHING you can say that will make me hurt more than I hurt already, Bobby. Nothing.

BOBBY. *(pause)* I wish I felt sorry for you. I wish I felt… anything. But I don't. I can't. I can't stand to look at you. I can't stand to be around you and if I had found this out and he wasn't sick, I'd…

KATE. What were you going to say?

BOBBY. Never mind.

KATE. I need to go.

(She rushes into the house.)

BOBBY. Shit –

(Family room/kitchen. **KATE** *grabs her purse and does an about face.)*

GRACIE. Mom –

KATE. Not now, Gracie. I'll be back later. Eat. Just eat some dinner. I'll be back. I have to –

(She exits.)

(Porch. **KATE** *rushes past* **BOBBY**.*)*

BOBBY. Katie, I'm sorry.

KATE. Don't touch me! And I'm Kate, remember?

BOBBY. I shouldn't have –

KATE. Yeah, well, you did! *(Pause. Tears.)* And we can't take back our actions, Bobby.

(She travels on. The car starts as **BOBBY** *watches her drive off, tires squealing.)*

BOBBY. Shit. *(kicks the bench)* Shit!

*(***BOBBY** *rushes into the house.)*

(Family room/kitchen. **BOBBY** *rushes over, takes his keys from the key tree, grabs his wallet and cell phone off of a table.)*

BOBBY. I'm going after your mom. She shouldn't drive this upset.

GRACIE. I'm coming with you.

BOBBY. No, Gracie, we're fighting and…not now –

GRACIE. *(bursting into tears)* That's all I ever hear anymore! Nobody listens to me or lets me do anything. It's worse than when he was well! It's all about Dayne and never about me and I'm worried about my mommy!

BOBBY. Okay, okay. Come on. Kendall, I have my cell. Look in on Dayne and call me if you need –

KENDALL. Don't worry, Dad. I'll handle everything here.

(BOBBY and GRACIE exit. KENDALL returns to the kitchen, drains the mac and cheese, stirs in sour cream and the cheese packet. He tastes it, then adds salt and pepper. Tastes again.)

Yum.

(He goes offstage, returns with a tray. He pulls out a bowl, fills it with the mac and cheese, grabs a napkin and fork, heads upstairs.)

(Dayne's room. KENDALL enters.)

KENDALL. *(whispers)* Dayne.

(Dayne doesn't stir. KENDALL puts the tray on the bed, shakes DAYNE gently.)

Dayne –

(DAYNE stirs.)

DAYNE. I was having a dream.

KENDALL. Was it that buried alive one?

DAYNE. No…it was…a good one. *(smiles)* I was making out with Shannon Burns.

KENDALL. She's really pretty. She sits by me in Algebra. And she wears really great shoes.

DAYNE. *(struggling)* I've always…wanted to…make out with her. She's hot. But I…I never had the nerve…to ask her out.

KENDALL. *(laughs)* Dayne, *everybody*…well, you know, all the girls, want to make out with *you*. I made you mac and cheese. You need to eat.

DAYNE. I try. It's…hard. Hey, could you do me a favor?

KENDALL. Sure, of course.

DAYNE. See, that trophy? The third one from the right? "First Team, All State." Just last year…could you line it up…with the others…it's…out of line.

(**KENDALL** *moves it back.*)

KENDALL. There, perfect.

DAYNE. Thanks –

KENDALL. You said mac and cheese was your favorite, so I made it for you. It's my very special mac and cheese. I use sour cream instead of butter and milk. You can't lose any more weight, Dayne. Please, eat.

DAYNE. I look awful…

KENDALL. No –

DAYNE. I know I do. I'm so…I'm not strong. None of those girls…would want me…if they could see how awful I look all yellow…and my stomach all pooched out. I look like a…shriveled, pregnant banana. Feel my bicep. It's not…there anymore.

KENDALL. *(feels)* It's still…kinda there. Come on. Eat my mac and cheese.

(**KENDALL** *takes a fork full and feeds it to* **DAYNE.** *He struggles to swallow it.*)

DAYNE. It's good. Mom still…mad…at Dad?

KENDALL. There's some tension, yes. But they'll work it out. Here, have another bite.

DAYNE. No. But it's…good. Maybe later.

KENDALL. I wish you would eat. I'm worried.

DAYNE. I'm sorry Dad brought…your mom. Did it…upset you?

KENDALL. A little. But your dad…Dad was just trying to –

DAYNE. Yeah, I know. I don't think it worked. The healing. I don't think it worked.

(silence)

KENDALL. I've been thinking about our musical –

DAYNE. It was a joke, Ken. Besides, this one doesn't seem to…have a happy ending.

KENDALL. No, it does! You'll get the transplant, there'll be this big rousing finale called "Delivered" – the title song. Funny, yet poignant and –

DAYNE. You're a funny little dude, Ken. All musicals… should have…happy endings.

KENDALL. Well, this one will. But they all don't. My favorite one doesn't.

DAYNE. Tell me about it. Tell me…about your favorite musical. You know…like a bedtime story. Mom used to…make me fall asleep.

KENDALL. Okay, but I'm warning you. The ending is not happy.

DAYNE. Yes –

KENDALL. Okay, sure. It's called "*Kiss of the Spider Woman*". It's so sad. So desperately tragic. I mean, I've never seen it, but I saw the movie. They're both based on a book. Me and Gracie watched it on cable. And I read the entire musical and ordered the original cast recording. It's brilliant. Won the Tony for Best Musical and everything else. Terrence McNally wrote the book and Kander and Ebb wrote the music. They are musical geniuses, responsible for a little musical called *Cabaret*. And another one called *Chicago*. And *Kiss of the Spider Woman*, of course.

DAYNE. Tell me…the story…

KENDALL. Oh, right. Well, it's very complicated. It's set in a jail. Somewhere in South America. Maybe Central. Not sure. And "Molina"… a role I plan to play someday, hopefully in the revival on Broadway… falls in love with his cellmate "Valentine". See, Molina has all these fantasies, you know, to pass the time in jail and we see them. The audience. And they are about a pretend famous actress. She exists only in the world of the play, see but not in real life. Her name is "Aurora". And she's captivating. Chita Rivera played her on Broadway and she was also in the original version of *Chicago*. It was such a coup to get her back in a Kander and Ebb musical and she won the Tony. She was nominated, didn't win for *Chicago* –

DAYNE. The story –

KENDALL. Sorry. I tend to get sidetracked. So anyway, well, Molina loves all her roles that he fantasizes about, but one scares him. *(very theatrical)* It's the role of a spider woman. Who kills with a kiss. So, at the end of the musical, Molina gets released and before he leaves he professes his love for Valentine and there is this song... and oh Dayne, it's so beautiful and sad called "Anything For Him". And when Molina sings, *(spoken)* "Please God, let him turn around and look at me." *(emotional)* But see, Valentine doesn't feel the same way, he likes women, but he uses Molina by kissing him to get Molina to make some phone calls outside of prison to people, Valentine's criminal cohorts that the authorities are after. And Molina does it, but it costs him his life because the authorities try to make him name names and he won't because of his loyalty to Valentine. And they bring him to the cell and in front of Valentine, they shoot him! And then the spider woman appears and kisses him. The kiss of death.

DAYNE. I don't like this musical.

KENDALL. Tragedy, drama, comedy and music. A perfect combination.

DAYNE. *(kidding)* You like it...cause two dudes kiss –

KENDALL. I do not! I like it because it's...you know, art.

DAYNE. It's cool, Ken. You know...I'm cool with it. With you.

KENDALL. *(nods)* What's it like, Dayne? To kiss someone.

DAYNE. You've never kissed anyone?

KENDALL. Just old people at the rest home with really bad breath. And my mom.

DAYNE. And that wasn't fun?

KENDALL. Not so much.

DAYNE. *(thinks)* So…you've never kissed someone you liked?

KENDALL. No. And it's certainly not going to happen in Vicksburg, Mississippi. I'll have to wait 'til I move to New York.

(Long pause. **DAYNE** *just stares at* **KENDALL** *for a moment, then with great effort, he reaches up and takes the back of* **KENDALL**'s *head and slowly pulls him down.)*

KENDALL. What are you doing?

*(***DAYNE*** kisses him. Lightly on the lips.)*

DAYNE. It's not fair…that you have to wait 'til you move to New York. Life…is not…fair, Kendall.

KENDALL. *(tears in his eyes)* I know.

DAYNE. I'm tired. Gonna…nap. Thanks for the…mac and cheese and that…uplifting bedtime story.

KENDALL. *(weak smile)* You're welcome.

*(***KENDALL*** takes the tray and starts out.)*

DAYNE. Hey, Kendall. Always remember…Dayne Westmoreland was your first kiss.

KENDALL. I'll never forget. Never.

(blackout)

(in blackout)

(voice-over) (singing) "When peace, like a river, attendeth my way, When sorrows like sea billows roll; Whatever my lot, Thou has taught me to say, It is well, it is well, with my soul. It is well, with my soul, It is well, with my soul, It is well, it is well, with my soul."

MINISTER. *(voice-over)* Thank you, Kendall. That was beautiful. We are here on this beautiful fall day to celebrate the life of Robert Dayne Westmoreland, Jr. There is nobody on this earth who is perfect, but God gives us a few who are near. And that was our Dayne. A bright, shining light that faded far too quickly…"

Scene Four

(Lights come up on the porch where **TIMOTHEA** *sits on the bench as the sun sets. She holds a Pyrex dish covered with foil that houses macaroni and cheese, and she is humming a hymn. A car drives up and four doors slam.* **KATE**, **BOBBY**, **GRACIE**, *and* **KENDALL** *walk up in silence, all in funeral attire.* **TIMOTHEA** *rises, weakly smiles at* **KENDALL**, *walks over to* **KATE**, *hands her the dish.)*

TIMOTHEA. It's just some comfort food. Nothing fancy. Matthew Mark's favorite. Macaroni and cheese. I use sour cream instead of butter and milk.

KATE. *(pause)* Thank you.

TIMOTHEA. God bless you all.

(She starts to exit and turns back.)

I didn't salt it…just in case…so you may have to salt it yourself. I'm sorry, Kate Westmoreland. To all of you. I pray that our Lord and Savior will comfort you all in this time of bereavement. I know what it's like to lose a child. It hurts like no other hurt.

BOBBY. We appreciate this gesture, Sister Timothea…we really do. I think we all need to go inside now and just –

TIMOTHEA. Yes, of course, Bobby Westmoreland. You are in my prayers. You are such a good father. You did all you could…all that was humanly possible.

BOBBY. I appreciate that. Come on, kids.

*(***BOBBY*** starts to lead ***KENDALL*** and ***GRACIE*** into the house.)*

KATE. I'll be right in. Kendall, could you take this in the house and put it in the refrigerator.

KENDALL. Yes, ma'am.

*(***BOBBY*** and ***GRACIE*** enter the house as ***KENDALL*** takes the covered dish from ***KATE***, starts to enter the house, but is stopped in the doorway by –)*

TIMOTHEA. Matthew Mark – ?

KENDALL. Yes, ma'am – ?

TIMOTHEA. I could have done better. And for that I am truly sorry.

KENDALL. Okay –

TIMOTHEA. I know you are happy with this family…but please…do not forget the foundation that I have instilled upon you. Your house is built on rock and not sand. *(off silent response)* I would like to give you a hug. May I, please?

(Family room. **BOBBY** *and* **GRACIE** *exit up the stairs.)*

(Porch. **KATE** *walks over and gives* **KENDALL** *a little hug, as if to give him permission to let his mother hug him.)*

KENDALL. Yes, ma'am.

*(***KATE** *backs away as* **TIMOTHEA** *rushes over and hugs* **KENDALL** *in the doorway from behind.* **KENDALL** *never turns around, doesn't hug back. He breaks away, closes the door and enters –)*

(Family room/kitchen. **KENDALL** *stands there for a moment, then walks over and places the macaroni and cheese on the counter, stares at it for another moment, then exits up the stairs.)*

(On porch. **TIMOTHEA** *lingers. Awkward silence as* **KATE** *reaches behind the plant, finds her cigarettes and lighter.)*

KATE. Please don't judge me. It's been the hardest day of my life.

TIMOTHEA. "Judge not, that ye be not judged." Matthew 7:1. I believe that we are both guilty of the violation of that scripture, Kate Westmoreland.

*(***KATE** *lights her cigarette, takes a drag, stares at* **TIMOTHEA.***)*

KATE. I agree.

TIMOTHEA. *(pause)* God bless you, Kate Westmoreland.

(**TIMOTHEA** *starts to exit.*)

KATE. *(calling after her)* How did you know? About my sin?

TIMOTHEA. The Lord spoke to me.

KATE. Was he specific? Did you know exactly what – ?

TIMOTHEA. No. We all sin, Kate Westmoreland –

KATE. So, could it have just been a good guess?

(**TIMOTHEA** *stares at* **KATE** *for a moment, indicates bench.*)

TIMOTHEA. Oh, no. May I?

(**KATE** *nods,* **TIMOTHEA** *heads over.*)

(*Dayne's room.* **GRACIE** *opens the door, enters and looks around, settling on the trophies and then on Dayne's football jersey laid over the pillow of his bed. She sits on the bed and continues to stare at the trophies as* **TIMOTHEA** *sits on the bench.*)

(*Porch.* **TIMOTHEA** *sits on the bench and takes* **KATE**'s *hand.*)

TIMOTHEA. We all sin, Kate Westmoreland. And the Lord will forgive you if only you will ask. But you must ask for forgiveness.

KATE. *(sudden tears, almost a gasp)* I have. You have no idea.

TIMOTHEA. So have I. But you...*we* must forgive ourselves. They say that's when the true healing will begin.

(*Also in tears, she looks over at the door where* **KENDALL** *wouldn't hug her.*)

And I don't know how to do that either.

(**KATE** *quickly wipes her eyes, stares at* **TIMOTHEA**. *Compassion envelops her entire being. She then reaches over and hugs* **TIMOTHEA**. **TIMOTHEA** *doesn't know how to respond, but then hugs her back, hard.* **TIMOTHEA** *breaks the hug and stands.*)

I am so sorry about Dayne. I know your heart is shattered. Please...please...take care of my son. Take care of...Kendall.

(She suddenly rushes away.)

KATE. *(quietly)* I will.

*(**KATE** continues to sit and stare.)*

*(Dayne's room. **BOBBY**, having lost his jacket and tie, passes Dayne's open bedroom door and sees **GRACIE** still staring at Dayne's trophies.)*

BOBBY. What are you doing, angel face? You okay?

*(**GRACIE** bursts into tears.)*

GRACIE. I wanted to…I wanted to tell him that I was sorry, Daddy.

BOBBY. Oh honey. *(sits on bed)* For what?

GRACIE. I messed up his trophies and all of his other stuff all the time…before he got sick. I did it…just to be mean…because he was too perfect…and I wasn't. I was a terrible sister, Daddy.

BOBBY. No –

GRACIE. I just thought…if…that if I said I was sorry for everything…that he would think…that I thought he was going to die. And I didn't, Daddy. I thought that it'd all be better. That you…that Mommy…could make it all better like when you kissed my boo-boos when I was little. And we didn't. And…he died not knowing that I was sorry for…all that. I just never thought he would die, Daddy.

BOBBY. Me either, angel face. But he did and we…have to – Do you realize how entertaining you were to your brother?

*(**GRACIE** shakes her head "no".)*

Dayne lived for your…your outbursts and everything you did…like rearranging his trophies.

*(**KENDALL** passes the door and looks in on **GRACIE** and **BOBBY** talking. He continues on and stops at the top of the stairs.)*

GRACIE. Really?

BOBBY. Yes. You entertained him. You gave him a gift. You are a gift, Gracie. To Dayne…to all of us. Dayne would have never wanted you to apologize…he really just wanted to live…so you could entertain him some more.

(GRACIE looks up at her dad, then gets up, goes over and rearranges Dayne's trophies.)

(Family room/kitchen/stairs.)

(KENDALL spots the macaroni and cheese and has an idea. He uncovers the dish and scoops macaroni and cheese into bowls, then salts each bowl with fervor.)

KENDALL. Dad…Mom…Gracie, come here!!

(Dayne's room.)

GRACIE. There.

BOBBY. *(chuckles)* That's my girl.

(Family room/kitchen. **KENDALL** *puts spoons into the bowls, picks two of them up.)*

KENDALL. Dad…Gracie!

(Dayne's bedroom/landing/stairs. **BOBBY** *gets up, puts his arm around* **GRACIE**, *leads her out of the room.)*

BOBBY. C'mon. Let's go see what…Kendall wants.

(They head down the stairs.)

(Family room/kitchen. **KENDALL** *meets* **BOBBY** *and* **GRACIE** *at the bottom of the stairs and hands them each a bowl, then rushes out the front door.)*

KENDALL. Mom…come in, I have a surprise.

(Porch. **KATE** *gets up and walks into the house.)*

(Family room/kitchen. **KENDALL** *rushes into the kitchen and grabs the two other bowls.)*

GRACIE. What are we doing?

KENDALL. You'll see.

(He hands a bowl to **KATE**, *keeps one.)*

KENDALL. *(cont.)* See, like…well, in the movies, they always toast to someone with champagne or something to drink and…well, I just thought…since Dayne loved mac and cheese…like me…that we could make a toast to Dayne…with it.

KATE. Well, I think that's a great idea.

GRACIE. It's ridiculous!

BOBBY. No, it's…perfect.

GRACIE. We're toasting with noodles!

KENDALL. Dad…will you make it…the toast?

BOBBY. Sure. *(thinks, lifts his bowl, then to **GRACIE**)* I have to admit, it is a little weird. Okay, everybody lift your bowl to toast…Robert Dayne Westmoreland, Jr. *(looks to heaven)* We honor your beautiful life, son. We are so glad – *(pause, looks at **KATE**, fighting emotion)* That you came to us. That you chose us. Our brother. Our son.

(They all awkwardly "click" bowls.)

KENDALL. Okay, now everybody eat a bite! You know, instead of drinking.

*(Everybody does. **KATE** continues to look at **BOBBY**. A long moment of them just staring at each other. **KATE** breaks the stare, turns and spots something out the window.)*

KATE. Oh, Bobby, look – *(She puts her bowl down.)* It's a full moon.

(She walks out the front door.)

*(**BOBBY** puts his bowl down, follows her.)*

*(Family room/kitchen. **GRACIE** goes over to **KENDALL**, who puts his arm around her as they stare at **BOBBY** and **KATE**.)*

*(Porch. **BOBBY** reaches **KATE**, stares at the moon as lights begin to fade.)*

KATE. You always did love a full moon.

(**BOBBY** *puts his arm around his wife, pulls her to him and kisses her head.*)

(*blackout*)

THE END

PROPERTY PLOT

Act One Presets

Porch: Newspaper, Lighter, Kate's Cigarettes

Living Room: On piano – Gracie's music book

Kitchen: Dayne's Playbook, Bananas, Peanut butter, Bread, Coffee mug, Pan with pre-cooked eggs, Plate with pre-heated biscuits, Pre-cooked bacon, Plates, Bowls, Silverware, Ice cream scoop, Coffeemaker with coffee, Telephone, Orange Juice, Jelly, Mustard, Roast Beef, Bottled Water, Paper Towels

Dayne's Bedroom: Trophies; Stack of boxers in dresser; Act I, Scene 2 stack of clothes; Alarm clock

Offstage: Anniversary bag present; T-shirt for Dayne to put on at breakfast, Squirt Bottle – to wet Dayne's hair after shower, Towel, Kendall's sheet music, Kate's cellphone, Bobby's cellphone, Kate's keys, Bobby's keys, Kate's purse, Gracie's purse, Gracie's cellphone, Pile of clothes for Dayne's laundry, Oklahoma flyer, Timothea's Bible, Pen, Computer, Pad of paper

Act I Grocery Bag: Weight gain powder, Vitamins, Ice Cream

Act Two Presets

Living Room: Add clutter – Mail stack, Magazines on table, Newspapers on the floor

Dayne's Bedroom: Balloons, Welcome Home poster, Basket of medicine bottles, Pill to swallow, Bottle of water with straw, Bell

Offstage: Timothea's dish of cooked mac and cheese

Act II Grocery Bag: Mac and Cheese box, Paper plates, Paper cups

COSTUME PLOT

Act One, Scene One

DAYNE: Boxers

KATE: Red halter dress, Silver heels, Silver wrap/scarf, Wedding band/engagement ring

BOBBY: Cream khakis, Navy polo with cream stripes, Black loafers, Black leather belt, Wedding band

Act One, Scene Two

KATE: Chocolate silk tank, Cream/brown print skirt, 3/4 sleeve chocolate jacket with matching wide belt, Brown sandal pumps

GRACIE: Navy polo, Navy/black/white plaid school uniform skirt, White ankle socks, White Keds

BOBBY: Royal blue/white thick-striped polo, Khakis, tennis shoes, Matching royal blue "Bobcats" baseball cap

KENDALL: Navy undershirt, Washed-out gray polo, Faded gray corduroy pants, Worn sneakers, Second-hand backpack

DAYNE: Same boxers, Navy Adidas track pants, Ole Miss sleeveless t-shirt, Royal blue football jersey with "Westmoreland" printed on the back with the number 84

Act One, Scene Three

TIMOTHEA: Brown turtleneck, Denim jumper, Knee-high stockings, Brown lace-up loafers

KATE: Jeans, Gray/brown tank, Cream sneakers w/brown stripes, Cantaloupe hoodie

BOBBY: Same as Act 1, Scene 2 – Add matching royal blue "Bobcats" windbreaker

KENDALL: Same as Act 1, Scene 2 – Add gray hoodie

GRACIE: Same as Act 1, Scene 2 – Add denim patchwork jacket; After exit, she changes into: Pink T-shirt, Gray cutoff sweatpants, Ankle socks

DAYNE: Designer jeans, T-shirt, Hoodie, Sneakers, Backpack

Act One, Scene Four

KENDALL: Light blue western shirt, Light brown wranglers, Suede chaps with dark brown fringe, Western belt with buckle, Suede vest, Cowboy hat, Cowboy boots

GRACIE: Magenta "Aunt Eller" dress with cream lace accents, Pink crocheted shawl, Black ankle boots, Gray wig, Wire-rimmed glasses

TIMOTHEA: Forest green turtle neck, Green/navy plaid jumper, Knee-high stockings, Brown lace-up shoes

Act One, Scene Five

BOBBY: Red Ole Miss T-shirt, Tan sweat pants, Slippers

KATE: Pale yellow/cream robe with matching slippers

Act Two, Scene One

KATE: Pale orange pullover, Jeans, Cream sneakers with brown stripes

DAYNE: Blue "American University" T-shirt, Navy sweat pants, White tube socks

BOBBY: Maroon polo, Jeans, Sneakers

GRACIE: Magenta/pink floral print dress, Matching headband, Gray leather jacket, Silver flats, Silver necklace

KENDALL: Gray/purple argyle T-shirt, Hoodie, Jeans, Converse sneakers

TIMOTHEA: Brown turtleneck, Tan jumper, Knee-high stockings, Oatmeal cardigan sweater, Brown lace-up loafers

Act Two, Scene Two

KATE: Pale yellow/cream robe with matching slippers

BOBBY: Blue/gray T-shirt, Tan sweatpants, Slippers

Act Two, Scene Three

TIMOTHEA: Floral printed prairie blouse, Green/gray jumper, Knee-high stockings, Brown lace-up loafers

BOBBY: Maroon sweatshirt, Jeans, Sneakers

DAYNE: Large white T-shirt, Navy sweatpants, Bloated abdomen pouch

KATE: Jeans, Sneakers, Dark brown camisole, Light brown corduroy coat with built-in hoodie

KENDALL: Tan khakis, Black converse sneakers, Light gray pullover (undershirt), Navy polo, Hoodie

GRACIE: Gray polo, School uniform skirt, Black leggings, White ankle socks, White Keds, Light pink winter coat with fur-trimmed collar

Act Two, Scene Four

TIMOTHEA: Dark purple floral print prairie dress with crocheted vest, Knee-high stockings, Brown slip-on loafers

BOBBY: Black suit, Black button-up shirt, Black tie, Black loafers

KENDALL: Black suit, Black button-up shirt, Black tie with purple accent, Black loafers

GRACIE: Black dress, Black lace cardigan, Silver chain

KATE: Black dress, Black pumps, Silver locket

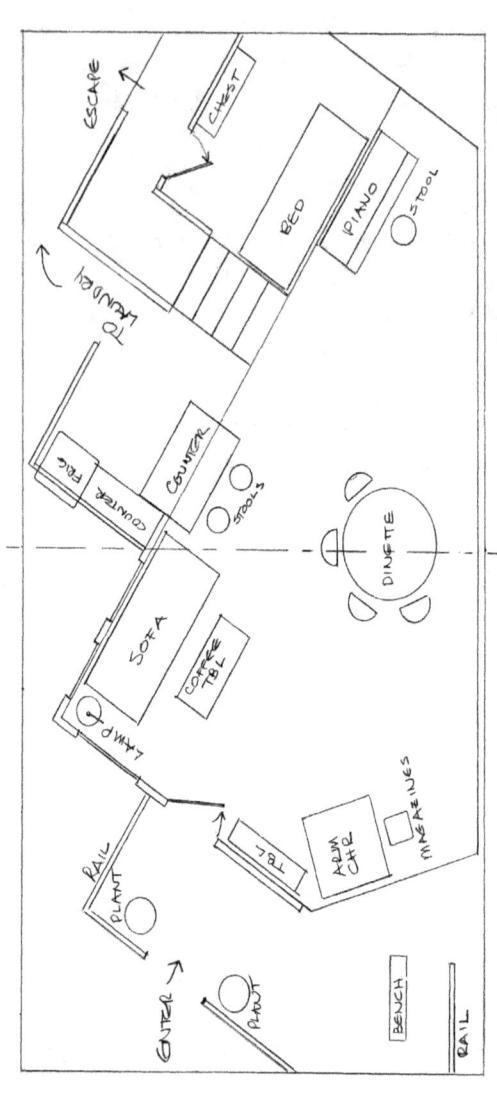

*Set design by Robert Steinberg

www.ingramcontent.com/pod-product-compliance
Lightning Source LLC
Chambersburg PA
CBHW071411290426
44108CB00014B/1771